still together

For my daughter, Taylah.

still together

CONNECTION
THROUGH MEDITATION

MANOJ DIAS

Hardie Grant

BOOKS

Contents

Introduction

Your parents and your teachers – bless them – probably had this absurd idea that when you grew up, you would know how to be an adult. You would know how to build healthy relationships, look after your finances, maybe raise children, and lead a successful life – all by yourself.

What they didn't teach you about was the pain of failed love, the burden of mortgage repayments and the scary new world of social media. They gave you titbits of wisdom, sure. But for many of us, our early childhood teachers didn't teach us how to understand doubt, fear, stress or our subconscious thoughts. They were probably still trying to understand their own.

I never learned that connection was a biological imperative, or that a profound lack of it would cause me to question my existence, my purpose, my value to this world. That lack drove me to binge eat, abuse drugs and hurt the people closest to me. It would ultimately drive me towards addiction, eating disorders and chronic and severe cases of generalised anxiety.

Many of us have experienced moments of anxiety.

What if I make an idiot of myself at the party? Will I make it in time for the meeting? What if I messed up that presentation? Did I lock the car?

Sometimes anxiety is fleeting and manageable. It's uncomfortable at the time, but it doesn't hang around for too long. For some, however, the anxiety we experience is chronic and debilitating. It's the kind of anxiety that doesn't go away, even when we see that we did lock the car, and that yes, the heating is turned off.

This kind of anxiety can stop us from leaving the house. It can affect our sleep, our health and our capacity to function at our best. It's a toxic, persistent presence that can ruin careers, relationships and lives. I know this, because it did these things to me.

For over ten years, I operated on low levels of anxiety without realising it. I assumed that the nerves and edginess came with having a corporate career. I supplemented my poor sleep with multiple cups of coffee, my afternoon lulls with chocolate, and my ever-growing self-doubt with procrastination. I had no idea that I had anxiety because I had no idea what it was. I remained completely unaware that I had anxiety until the day I had a panic attack at work.

I remember it well. I was enjoying my morning coffee, but noticed that it felt a little strong. Damn strong, actually – the kind that feels like it's gone straight into your bloodstream. My hands began to tremble. My heart raced, a wave of emotion consumed me and my bottom lip started quivering. My first thought was,

STILL TOGETHER

'I can't let the fellas see this'. But my colleagues did see, of course. I'm sure it was hard not to notice when I got up from my desk gasping for air. I ran out of the office hyperventilating, and started pacing the busy city streets.

I knew then that it wasn't the damn coffee. It was some kind of anxiety attack – the kind that had probably been bubbling away for months, maybe even years. So I did what any sane person on the verge of a nervous breakdown would do. I quit my job and I didn't leave the house for months.

I saw a lot of experts during that time. Doctors, psychiatrists, shamanic healers and reiki masters all listened to my story and did their best to help me. By this point I had developed a severe anxiety disorder, chronic insomnia and a prescription medication addiction from a misdiagnosed case of ADHD. I felt like I was freefalling. I was clinging to anything and everything for sanity, but nothing caught, and I just kept plunging further into the void. Then one day, a Buddhist meditation teacher changed my life. What he said to me was fairly simple, but it resonated like nothing ever had before.

'You are not your thoughts.'

Those five little words were like a magic potion, and this revelation is what served as my introduction to Buddhist meditation. Although I was born in Sri Lanka and raised in a Buddhist household, meditation was never a part of my parents' practice. But this humble, wise Buddhist meditation teacher taught me that the wisdom to understand my suffering had been within me all along. I had the ability to train my mind and heart to connect to the present moment, see things as they really are and, in turn, connect fully with life.

I studied with my teacher, whom I still lovingly refer to as Guruji (spiritual teacher), daily for eight years. In that time I attended countless silent meditation retreats, devoured as many books as I could and travelled the world exploring mindfulness and Buddhism. At one point I considered taking robes and heading back to Sri Lanka to become a monk. However, I knew I would miss the football – and, more importantly, my daughter. I had no intention of becoming a teacher; the idea wasn't even on my radar.

But when I returned to my corporate life, I felt a deep sense of emptiness. My life felt bereft of meaning and purpose. What I had yearned for so deeply in my youth – money, career growth, fancy experiences – I no longer craved. One day, my teacher said he was not feeling well and asked me to take over and teach his class. It was a set-up, of course – he wanted to challenge me to try my hand at teaching. Nervous but hopeful, I taught my first class in front of my teacher, much to his delight. A few weeks afterwards, I felt called to commence a great journey, one that could not promise stability or wealth, but one that would make me rich in compassion and connection. So, with a young daughter and only a small amount of money, I left my familiar, comfortable life behind and stepped into the unknown.

For me, meditation was the key to understanding my pain and my experience. It taught me to observe my thoughts without necessarily accepting them as facts. It taught me that my mind was a muscle, and that in the same way as we work to strengthen our arms or legs at the gym, my mind could be strengthened, and trained to focus on the present moment. When you focus on the present moment, the surrounding noise and chatter falls away and you can handle with grace and wisdom whatever experience you are thrown. This was meditation: a tool to help me feel more connected to life.

My hope for this book is that you, too, will begin to reclaim your humanity and your intrinsic ability to form and nurture connections with genuine warmth and tenderness. We live in anxious times. We disconnect from each other based on our political and social beliefs, our fear of being truly seen, our time constraints and our lifestyles. This book will offer you insight, from a mindfulness and Buddhist perspective as well as from lessons gleaned along my own journey, and from many of the countless students I have taught over the decade. Much of what I'll share with you, you may already know. It will resonate in the deepest part of you.

My greatest wish is that you make the most of this precious human life. Mindfulness, compassion and meditation are the tools that can help you do that and, if practised regularly, these things will lead to a lifetime of deeper connections and greater fulfilment.

With love,
Manoj

THE AGE OF DISCONNECTION

∞

CHAPTER ONE

∞

Do you ever wonder how you got to this point in your life? Do you find yourself thinking:

Is this really it? Is this how the rest of my life is going to play out? Why do I feel so disconnected from everything and everyone?

Too many of us go through life like this, in a perpetual state of lack, and functioning on autopilot. Life feels like Groundhog Day, like something that just happens to us, something over which we have little control. We try to manage our health, relationships and careers in a world that demands more and more of us, and we question when, if ever, we will get off this hamster wheel – a hamster wheel we don't even remember getting on in the first place.

WHY AM I SO DISCONNECTED?

Technology, and even social media, can be wonderful and valuable tools. For many of us it's impossible to imagine life without our gadgets. We can send emails to friends and colleagues, speak to people on the other side of the world, do our banking, order food and find a lover, all from the palm of our hand. Our devices can make us more efficient, and in many ways they make our lives easier. But it's hard to miss the impact technology is having on human (dis)connection.

Many of us spend a huge chunk of our time looking at our phones – scrolling through social media, checking emails or watching TikToks. We do this instinctively, even when we don't need to – even when we're waiting 90 seconds for our coffee, when our minds wander during lunch, when a stressful thought enters our mind. We seek solace in our phone so automatically we barely know we're doing it and, though we may not realise it, what we're actually doing is disconnecting from the present moment.

We've all spoken to someone at work, at home or during our day who we know is not mentally present. They might be talking to you, but they're not fully engaged in the conversation. Maybe they're thinking about what to eat for lunch or remembering the bills they have to pay, or perhaps they're working through their own emotions about something. But, whatever the reason is,

EXERCISE

Take a moment now to consider your day
so far, right up until you read this paragraph.
Consider the following questions:

∞

What did you do five minutes ago?

How did you wake up?

What sort of interactions did you have with
the people in your life this morning?

When was the last time you had a truly deep
and meaningful conversation?

When was the last time you felt at ease waiting
for your coffee by yourself, without needing to
bury your head in your phone?

STILL TOGETHER

they're not really *there* and you know it. You probably do the same thing yourself from time to time.

We live in a world where innovation promises to keep us more up-to-date and connected, but all too often, many of us feel the exact opposite. We experience life in the same way we experience a drive to the supermarket – we're barely aware of which streets we crossed on the way, or how we even got there. Basically, we're on autopilot. Along the way, we miss moments of connection to the world around us, to each other and to ourselves. But we got there, right? That's the most important thing, isn't it?

The term 'attention economy' was coined when researchers noted our limited ability to keep up with the information being fired at us. American cognitive scientist Herbert Simon was one of the first to articulate the concept. In his book *Designing Organizations for an Information-rich World*, he said, 'In an information-rich world, the wealth of information means a dearth of something else: a scarcity of whatever it is that information consumes. What information consumes is rather obvious: it consumes the attention of its recipients.'

Social media, in particular, has a way of devouring our attention to the point where we forget about what's happening away from our screens, and that's because it's designed to affect us on a physiological level. When we pick up our phones to see a new email, DM or cat video, our brains get a hit of dopamine, the pleasure-producing neurotransmitter.

Whether it's taking a bite of delicious food, being intimate with another person or indulging in drugs or alcohol, pleasurable behaviours cause our brains to secrete this chemical and make us feel good, momentarily. The catch with dopamine is that the minute its effects wear off, we want – no, crave – more, quickly.

Interacting socially provides us with quick, repetitive doses of dopamine. So, whenever an anticipated email lands in our inbox or when our phones vibrate with a new social media notification, we're alerted to the fact that someone, somewhere is connecting with us, and this makes us feel good.

App designers have worked tirelessly to encourage us to check our phones as often as possible. None of us are immune to their strategies. I regularly fall victim to my subconscious need to be rewarded, whether it's the rush from an email I'm excited to receive or the urge to check how many people have liked my latest Instagram post.

It's addictive, but what we see on social media doesn't always have the desired, pleasurable effect.

We compare ourselves to others who are living their (seemingly) best lives in exotic places, wearing smug smiles and the latest designer gear. I have an internal narrative that pipes up whenever I see others doing 'better' than me. It tells me, *You need to do better*. It tells me that I am not enough. I feel like I need to work harder, exercise more, buy better clothes, find cooler friends and travel to more luxurious places. Of course, our psychology plays

EXERCISE

**Check in with your body and your mind
after scrolling through social media or
watching videos online.**

∞

Do you feel uplifted and energised?

How long does that feeling last?

Do you feel tension anywhere in your body?

Notice where.

Pay attention to the thoughts elicited
by what you see – are they pleasant,
unpleasant or neutral?

EXERCISE

To practise mudita, simply bring to mind
a person who has achieved something or ran
into some good fortune.

∞

Think of all the work they may have done to get
to that point and all the tears and hardships that
others may not have seen.

Now see this person happy and proud. To do this,
remember the feeling you had when you achieved
something, or maybe the feeling of being on holiday
or receiving a gift. See if you can now feel what this
person is feeling.

Feeling joy for others is at first a strange exercise.
We're not used to doing this in today's society, so it
can be hard. Over time, our jealousy and envy subsides
and we can feel a tangible connection to other
humans. We're reminded of our wish simply to be
well and do well.

a role in this – what we have or have not experienced in our life. That said, these days perhaps we can all relate to a scarcity mindset.

I've been working on an antidote to this that comes from a teaching from the Buddha: a heart practice called sympathetic joy, or mudita. Mudita is the practice of being happy for other people's happiness, genuinely and fully. It can seem easy, conceptually, but when we explore our own happiness and tendencies, we often begin to see that genuinely celebrating other people's happiness can be one of the most challenging things for us. Although many seasoned meditators might aim for mudita, we too often fall into the trap of feeling jealous and snarky, even though we have the capacity to feel otherwise. Without an awareness of the ways technology can affect us, it's easy to forget that we can control how we respond to it.

The real self vs.
the virtual self

Online, we are able to present a filtered, edited version of ourselves, the version that we want the world to see. If there's dissonance between your online persona and your real one, however, this can be an uncomfortable thing to try and reconcile.

When I first started teaching meditation, I was excited to share online the lessons that had been so transformational in my life. The desire to share these benefits with others drove me to study more and to share more via social media. Eventually, I started to notice that not all posts were received equally. Photos were getting more attention than long-winded and heartfelt captions, and I began to change what I wrote and the images I posted in order to get more likes and comments. I would check on these posts more and more often, eager to see how many people were responding to them. What started off as a weekly post became a daily post, followed by endless check-ins to see who had liked it.

I was flattered that people were interested in what I had to say and, more importantly, that they were interested in me. Or, at least, the version of me that I had presented to the world. But it became harder and harder to live up to that persona in real life. The calm, conscious and gentle Manoj portrayed on social media is just a small part of who I really am. As much as I strive to be more equanimous, I still get angry, binge eat burgers and fries when I'm emotional, and lose my temper at the people I love the most. I'm human.

Getting attached to a sense of self is fraught with danger. In Buddhist practice, the belief is that we're ever-changing, ever-evolving and that all we are is a blend of material form, feelings, perceptions and consciousness. There is no inherent self. But we tend to fixate on the idea of the self, especially when it comes to creating the self that we choose to present to the world.

What I learned many years ago through my meditation practice was that I was often using technology, specifically social media, to fill a void in my life. Sometimes that void was loneliness, other times it was a desire to be seen or heard. The more time I spent creating this idealised persona, the less time I was spending connected to life itself. Perhaps this resonates?

The challenges presented by social media may be most deeply felt by millennials, but disconnection caused by technology affects people of all ages. As we attempt to wrest back control of our minds and our bodies, it's vital to recognise that we alone hold the power to reconnect with ourselves and the world around us, in real time. Social media might be designed to capture our attention, but we can train our minds to resist it. If we can cultivate mindfulness, each moment offers us a choice between connection and disconnection, between what's real and tangible, and what only exists on screen.

What meditation practice
and mental training can
help us with is seeing
the impermanence of the
structured self. In doing so,
we can not be so attached
to it, and ease into our
being without an agenda.

Loneliness

Perhaps the question we should really be asking is: What is our addiction to technology really masking? It is simple and effective to assign blame to the addictive algorithms created by clever engineers, but why are we so vulnerable to their tactics?

According to research conducted by the Australian Psychological Society and Swinburne University, one in four Australians and three in five Americans experience loneliness. Loneliness has been a part of life since the dawn of time, and is not a mental health issue in itself – we all experience it at various times in our lives. However, being lonely increases our chances of poor mental health, and poor mental health increases our chances of experiencing loneliness.

We live in times where our biological need for human connection has been overtaken by an ideology of hyper-individualism. Perhaps it's a belief that we can accomplish anything if we put our minds to it, or catchy slogans like 'be your own boss' or 'you don't need anyone' that perpetuate these views. Ironically, we may believe that things like fame and wealth will deliver a sense of validation and perhaps even fill the void that our disconnection occupies. But it may be worth asking if the fame and wealth we so ardently strive for ultimately deliver what we really want – to be happy, healthy and free of suffering.

A study undertaken by Boston College's Center on Wealth and Philanthropy titled 'The joys and dilemmas of wealth' surveyed 165 households, 120 of which have at least US$25 million in assets. The respondents' average net worth was US$78 million, and two even reported being billionaires. Given that the joys of being super wealthy are pretty self-evident, the survey focused its attention on the woes associated with wealth. Interestingly, the results showed that the wealthiest responders tended to be largely dissatisfied with their lives. Why? Most of them said their wealth had caused them additional stress and anxiety, and had negatively impacted their work life, love life and, ultimately, their family life.

The journalist Graeme Wood writes in his piece in *The Atlantic* 'Secret fears of the super rich': 'A vast body of psychological evidence shows that the pleasures of consumption wear off through time and depend heavily on one's frame of reference. Most of us, for instance, occasionally spoil ourselves with outbursts of deliberate and perhaps excessive consumption: a fancy spa treatment, dinner at an expensive restaurant, a shopping spree. In the case of the very wealthy, such forms of consumption can become so commonplace as to lose all psychological benefit: constant luxury is, in a sense, no luxury at all.'

Basically, our craving for satisfaction never subsides. Even when we seemingly have everything that we need, there is a lingering dissatisfaction, and a belief that the elusive happiness we seek exists somewhere apart from where we are. It may be found in a new pair of shoes, a holiday package deal or in a new car, or it may cleverly disguise itself as a slimmer body or sharper mind. These messages are reinforced through television, radio and now on our smartphones, too. This constant thirst for more is a root cause of our suffering in the Buddhist world view.

It's no wonder so many of us feel isolated, lonely and lost. As it turns out, social isolation has been with us since long before COVID-19, through systems that have been designed to keep us separated, busy and productive.

My teacher Dr Miles Neale would refer to this as the hedonic treadmill of life. This treadmill feels like a conveyor belt of endless pleasurable, self-satisfying experiences that ultimately prove unsatisfying and don't take us anywhere. This is a culture that can breed competition.

In my early days of teaching, I would feel pangs of envy when I saw other teachers doing better than me. Many of the studios I worked with would constantly tell me I needed to do better. It would motivate me to work harder, to be smarter with my marketing and more strategic with my time. I now laugh at how much work I have done when it comes to dismantling such deep, intergenerational conditioning – and how much I still have left to do. So here we are, this mammalian, tribal species that once had to rely on each other to survive imminent threats and danger, and now we're pitted against the very people we once depended on to survive. Is productivity and achievement really more valuable than connection and love? Perhaps the great paradox is this: when we feel discomfort from loneliness and the agitation that inevitably arises as a result, we will do anything and everything we can to avoid feeling this way – so we turn back towards our smartphones and our televisions. We load up our online shopping carts and orientate our lives away from the very thing that will help us – each other.

Don't get me wrong, I love online shopping! And my smartphone, and especially television. I'm not suggesting you eradicate from your life everything you gain enjoyment from. Instead, much of this book will ask you to examine for yourself the many ways in which you may have disconnected from your own life. What thoughts, actions or beliefs motivate us to turn away from ourselves and each other? These questions and the subsequent answers will at times be uncomfortable. But consider them a challenge, and an invitation to reimagine the way you live, love, work and connect.

MEDITATION PRACTICE

This is an introductory reflection that invites us to tune into our bodies.

∞

1. Sit comfortably on a chair, cushion or a couch.

2. Make sure you're comfortable, but not too comfortable – you don't want to fall asleep.

3. Take a few deep breaths. Really notice your breath leaving your body.

4. After a few moments of noticing your breath, take a moment to reflect. *Where am I feeling disconnected in my life? Where do I want to feel more connected in my life?*

5. Allow the answers to arise intuitively, without questioning them. Try not to judge or 'work out' what's arising – feel how you feel without judgement.

STILL TOGETHER

Taking back control from technology

Turn off notifications

This one is a game-changer. Do we really need to be notified every time someone likes a photo or sends us an email? Once we turn off our notifications, we can be intentional about the apps we use instead of being seduced to check them all the time. Turn off all your non-critical notifications.

Practise being happy for other people

Let's be honest, all the people you see on social media who appear to have zero bad days are not really having zero bad days. We all have shitty days, we just don't tend to share them. Can you remember how nice it felt to see a friend of yours happy? Maybe they announced a new relationship or got a promotion. Can you recall how good that felt in your body? Research has shown that we benefit from these moments as if we were experiencing them. Cultivating happiness for others' happiness – real or perceived – is a far more productive and positive experience than allowing yourself to feel inferior or jealous.

Track your usage

These days, smartphone users can access data that tells us
how much time we're spending on our phones. This is often
delivered in the form of a weekly notification – and this
is one notification definitely worth checking. It's a handy,
sometimes sobering, reminder of all those hours you could
be spending doing other more important things, out there
in the real world.

Post honestly and post kindly

We all have the capacity to influence others immensely.
The way we look at someone and the things we say to
a person, even online, can shape the trajectory of their day.
A good ritual that I usually follow before posting is to check
in with what I'm feeling. Am I angry, sad, excited? This can
impact the language we use. Then I ask myself, what is my
intention? Is it to share something helpful or kind or amusing,
or is it to hurt someone or say something negative?

There's no need to overthink it, but take a second before you
post, and be mindful of posting solely for likes. This focus on
likes means you're posting as a reward-driven exercise rather
than sharing something without expectation.

Designate times for social media

Ever see a cool pair of shoes on Instagram and 30 minutes later find yourself on the profile of your ex-girlfriend's new boyfriend's best friend's new dog? Stop yourself from falling down the rabbit hole by limiting the amount of time you spend on certain apps. There are, ironically, apps to help you do just that.

Experiment with phone-free days

This one is a beauty. Do you think you could go an entire day without using your phone? Or, at the very least, without being online? Many of my students who have attempted this have reported how beneficial it is. We've been around for centuries and managed okay without the internet until fairly recently. This little experiment can help you feel more connected to things that technology can cause us to neglect, such as nature, other people and ourselves.

Take mindful moments while scrolling

Next time you catch yourself scrolling mindlessly on your
phone, take a moment to check back into the present
moment. A mindful moment is simply a moment we
bring awareness to. It could be noticing how our feet feel
against the floor, or tapping into how we feel as we're
scrolling. It could be as simple as taking three deep and
intentional breaths that break up the mindless scroll cycle,
momentarily unhooking us from our phones.

If you can speak to a real human, do it

Call instead of text, and meet for coffee instead
of sending an endless chain of WhatsApp messages.
Any chance you get to connect with someone more
authentically, take it. We love efficiency and we all seem
to be time poor. But it's a rare and radical act to connect
on a more personal level, and it's far more emotionally
and spiritually rewarding than the digital equivalent.

STILL TOGETHER

REIMAGINING
LIFE THROUGH
CONNECTION

∞

CHAPTER TWO

∞

Humans were born to connect. Long before we made our way into the world, we were each just a tiny peanut-shaped object inside our mother's womb, connected to her via an umbilical cord. We had to rely on her health for our own health; our connection to our mother was a life or death situation. When we exit the womb, we are reliant on the wisdom and knowledge of those who help us undergo that journey – doctors, nurses, doulas, elders. Without their care, we cannot survive.

In 1943 prominent psychologist Abraham Maslow was in search of meaning in his own life, when he developed a theory. He called it Maslow's hierarchy of needs, or Maslow's pyramid. This brilliant concept has gone on to shape many psychological studies and business programs, and has given purpose to countless lives. Maslow's pyramid outlines five types of human need. At the lowest level of the pyramid are the things we need to survive at our most basic level: food, air, water, sleep, clothing. Next up in the hierarchy are our safety needs: our health, employment, a safe place to live. And on the next rung up? The human need to belong and to feel connected to others. Right after food, water, a safe place to live and a job, what we need most to thrive as humans is to feel connected to other humans. We crave acceptance, love, romantic attachment and community, and we depend upon friendships, intimate connections and family to provide support and nurturing through the ups and downs of our modern, fast-paced and hyper-individualised lives.

Numerous studies have shown that the healthiest, happiest people tend to be the ones who have the deepest connections to friendship groups and their communities. In fact, in order to move through Maslow's pyramid from the bottom through to the middle (love and belonging) and then to the top (esteem needs such as appreciation, respect and self actualisation, secure and safe connections are a vital part of the process.

I'd go one step further
than Maslow and say
that connection might be
just as important to a
healthy, happy life as air
and water.

STILL TOGETHER

WHAT IS CONNECTION?

The word 'connection' suggests a relationship in which a person or thing is linked with someone or something else. In that sense, connection could mean any number of things. It may be our connection to our parents or our partner, or it could be our connection to our culture or religion. It could even be our connection to our Vitamix or couch! I want to focus on our connection to other humans, perhaps best described by author and professor Brené Brown in her book *The Gifts of Imperfection* as 'the energy that exists between people when they feel seen, heard, and valued; when they can give and receive without judgement; and when they derive sustenance and strength from the relationship.'

It's possible to be in a crowd of our closest friends or family and still feel disconnected. That's because what we truly, deeply want and need is not just to be around others, but to be *understood* by others, or, as Brené Brown puts it, 'to feel seen, heard and valued'.

In the Buddhist practice, connection is often taught through the concept of dependent origination, or the idea that all phenomena is interdependent, an idea often known as 'pratitya-samutpada'. Whatever is comes into existence because of factors and conditions created by other phenomena. This applies largely to mental and psychological factors, as well as to tangible and intangible things, seen and unseen, known and unknown, in our everyday life. This is a basic overview of the theory

'Whatever affects one directly,
affects all indirectly ... I can
never be what I ought to be
until you are what you ought
to be, and you can never
be what you ought to be until
I am what I ought to be.'

– Dr Martin Luther King

'Without a cloud, there
will be no rain; without rain,
the trees cannot grow;
and without trees,
we cannot make paper.'

– Thich Nhat Hanh

of dependent origination, one that we can examine by simply reflecting on what 'is' in our own lives that is connected to something or someone else.

Our functional existence depends on many things. The chair, couch or bed you are sitting on was sold to you by retail staff, shipped to the store by drivers, manufactured by workers, crafted by carpenters and conceptualised by designers. And before that? That wood was sourced from a tree, the tree was once a seed, and that seed needed water, rain and earth to thrive.

The phone you use, the bed that you sleep in, the coffee you purchase, the food that gets delivered to you. When we look around, we see the web of connections that exist in our lives. We see that independently of each other, some things just wouldn't work, or would not even exist. Take, for example, you. You wouldn't be here if your parents didn't have a connection. That connection led to another type of connection, and nine months later, there you were.

If Brené Brown's definition of connection resonates with you, think about how you could relate this to your own connection to yourself. Do you *see* yourself? Do you *hear* yourself? Do you *value* yourself?

Connecting to ourselves

It was the very first time I attended a yoga class that I realised how disconnected I was from my mind and body. As the teacher began to call out random sanskrit words that referred to postures (it seemed), I distinctly remember the feeling of looking like a clown. Actually, I felt more like a baby giraffe trying my best to stand up while others looked at me with judging eyes, most likely thinking, 'Who is this awkward dude and what is he doing here?' I was about two minutes into this negative spiral when I heard my teacher call out the words:

'Where are you, right now?'

Where was I? Well, I was plummeting into a rabbit hole of thoughts that revolved around me being a complete and utter misfit masquerading as a yogi while feeling sure that everyone in the room was laughing at me. Have you ever had moments like this? Lost in a vortex of stories and fantasies?

I realised at that moment that I wasn't sure when I had last felt connected to my body. I spent so much of my time in my head. Catastrophising, analysing, fantasising. No one in that yoga room was laughing at me. In all likelihood, no one was paying much attention to me at all. Chances were, they were all thinking the same thoughts about themselves – or thinking about something else entirely.

A 2005 National Science Foundation article reported that the average person has about 12,000 to 60,000 thoughts per day. Of those, 95 per cent are the exact same thoughts as the day before. And 80 per cent of those thoughts are negative.

If I was not there, connected to the present moment, my body and myself, where was I? I was lost in my own thoughts, worrying about what the people around me were thinking, feeling or doing. I have a feeling some of you can relate to this.

We tend to spend a lot of our time caught between past experience and future fears. We might be on a first date, and either worrying about making a good impression or anticipating that the whole thing will go badly, or it might be our first day at a new job, when we feel like we're going to be 'found out' as being incompetent. Whatever the situation is, odds are we are disconnected from our bodies, which are always firmly in the present moment. Instead, we are caught up in our minds, oscillating between future projections and past regrets. New situations are often accompanied by a soundtrack of negative thoughts. This constant soundtrack trains our minds to register negative stimuli more often and also to dwell on these moments, in turn making them seem bigger and more uncomfortable. It's why we tend to recall our pain more vividly than our happiest moments, and why we cling to negative feedback more tightly than to compliments. We feel what our brains perceive as negative much more deeply than we do praise or happiness.

Our own critical minds are often at work every time we look in a mirror. What we see staring back at us is a face or a person that needs improvement, whether that 'improvement' means fewer wrinkles or less fat and more muscles. Society has created a version of beauty that many of us, including myself, struggle to feel included in.

We so rarely look at our reflection in the mirror and see ourselves just as we are: beautiful and, more importantly, loveable.

These thoughts are so automatic and frequent that we may not even realise we are thinking them.

ACCEPT YOURSELF

What would it be like to love what we see in the mirror – and the mind and heart that goes with it?

∞

What if we saw the beauty in our wrinkles, the stories in our stretch marks and the love in our eyes? What if I was to tell you that it is possible to fall in love with yourself every morning? We've been conditioned to believe we should always be on the path to continuous improvement – so why not use this as a model for our own self-acceptance?

It IS possible to shift our focus from our weaknesses to our goodness. While we might be always growing and learning, we're fundamentally whole and complete, right now.

STILL TOGETHER

SELF-LOVE

Self-love is accepting that we are good and whole, even with our wounds and insecurities. In the Buddhist practice, we often refer to this as Buddha nature or basic goodness. It's the underlying sense that no matter what we have done or what we have been through, we are whole.

At the Wat Traimit temple in Bangkok, Thailand, there is a statue known as the Phra Phuttha Maha Suwana Patimakon – the Golden Buddha. This statue is a whopping 3.91 metres tall and 3.1 metres wide.

For many years, during raids by Burmese invaders in the 1700s, countless statues and figures were destroyed. But the sheer size of this particular statue, which was covered in thick concrete, meant that it lay untouched for many years, unable to be moved. Centuries later, the statue eventually found its way to Wat Traimit, where it was kept in a building hidden away from the other main statues. The monks diligently cleaned this concrete-covered statue daily until one day it was chipped in the process. Blinded by the light that shone beneath the concrete, the monks kept chipping away at the statue. After carefully removing the outer layer, what stood before them was this 500-tonne golden statue – the Golden Buddha.

To me, this story is a wonderful metaphor for the way we view ourselves. We often get so caught up with surface concerns on which we base our self-worth that we don't recognise the power and beauty lying dormant within us. Whether it was a bully at school, a parent who didn't encourage our growth or a society or culture that's made us feel like we are not enough, these experiences often leave us with some very negative beliefs about ourselves. But it doesn't have to be that way. We can override those unconscious beliefs and cultivate self-love and self-acceptance through our awareness and our practice.

The practice of meditation is a path of self-discovery, but also a path to uncovering our innate goodness. Goodness is the inherent quality of compassion and worthiness that lies beneath the countless stories we tell ourselves. Through meditation, we become familiar with ourselves in such an intimate and confronting way that over time and through training we develop a compassionate heart and a discerning mind. We gain compassion for our human experience, as flawed and imperfect as it might be, and we develop insight into the nature of our human experience.

We come to accept that experiences are impermanent, because everything is impermanent, therefore we can train our hearts and minds to stop getting so attached to what is continuously in flux. We can learn not to perceive things in a continuously negative way, and come to understand that we're not the only ones having these thoughts – therefore, we're not alone. Ultimately, we can find peace in the awareness that our conditioned thoughts and beliefs about our worthiness and value aren't true. We're whole just as we are, and we don't need to be fixed or improved.

When we can lower the masks we wear out in the world and refuse to be defined by the stories of our pain, trauma and conditioning, we can head courageously towards being our most authentic, vulnerable selves.

VIEW YOURSELF
WITH KINDNESS

Look in the mirror and see the beauty that
looks back at you. You might hear another voice
finding things to complain about; just notice it,
as it comes and goes.

∞

Your nose is perfect; it helps you breathe
in air that keeps you alive.

Your eyes have seen the world and the
world is contained within them.

Your mouth has spoken words of love
and words of anger.

You are a human. There is nothing to fix
or change or improve. There is only something
to learn from, accept and love.

What else do you admire about the image
in front of you?

STILL TOGETHER

Chapter Two

'OTHERNESS' – SEEING OURSELVES IN EACH OTHER

As we begin to cultivate our reconnection to our most authentic self, the long-held views we had about ourselves may start to slowly dismantle. This is a natural response to the consistent practice of opening our minds and hearts to our natural experience. We start to connect to a deeper sense of our bodies and, over time, develop a sense of empathy, connection and awareness towards other beings. Again, this is a natural response to our practice. As we begin to calm ourselves and settle a mind that is wandering and confused, and perhaps even in pain, we flex our brain's compassion regions. Over time, this builds not only an inner tenderness, but also a resilience. We may even have moments of spontaneous insight, perhaps when we're dancing or listening to a piece of beautiful music, where our sense of self is dissolved and we begin to feel part of something much bigger.

Many of us would liken this to a feeling of 'oneness' and a sense of deep, universal connection. This should be enjoyed and savoured, but also gently questioned. What are we one with? Who are we one with?

The answer is complicated and nuanced, because it depends on who you ask and what body that person exists in. Perspective, in this instance, matters, because that feeling of connection and the bliss you feel from a sense of oneness may be a privilege many don't get to experience. And that's okay, it shouldn't diminish your joy. The Buddha talked about the doctrine of two truths, where there can be two opposing viewpoints that are both true. This is widely discussed as the relative and the absolute truths. An absolute truth is that we are interconnected and not separate. But a relative truth is that we are all different. We are diverse, have varied experiences and, as a consequence of our relative differences, we experience life in contrasting ways. Some of us grow up and live with oppression, inequity and a lifetime of othering.

> 'Otherness' is defined as the quality or
> state of being other, or *different.*'

You may ask yourself how otherness exists within a world where connection is so important to each and every human.

Along with the many beautiful things there are on earth to savour and be delighted in, many of us unfortunately also experience sexism, racism, homophobia or transphobia, and xenophobia. We accentuate our differences and not our similarities, and in doing so we choose one truth over the other. We lean more into what separates us instead of what unites us. One person's desire to love someone of the same sex may be an attraction we don't share. Instead of seeing this as a mutual human desire for connection, we may choose to focus on how different their choice is to ours. The absolute truth is that we each just want to love and be loved. The relative truth is that our choices vary. Seeing both truths is a necessary skill when navigating our mental and physical wellness, but it is just as useful when negotiating our

When we speak of
oneness, we must begin
to explore the absolute
and the relative.

own negativity bias. At its best, otherness can help us feel deeply connected to one another, but at its worst, it creates a separation that can be felt across generations.

I was nine years old when I first told myself I was different. I was sitting in class and felt a ball of paper hit me in the back of the head. When I turned around, two young boys were sitting behind their desks, laughing, high-fiving each other and staring at me with what looked like hatred in their eyes.

'What are you looking at, *burnt toast?*'

'Burnt toast' was the first racial slur I experienced. There were countless more that followed. I grew up in a time where a 'boys will be boys' attitude prevailed, and racism was part of the cultural landscape. This is when I started to feel 'othered'. I felt that I was different and, as a result, was not included or welcome. I had never previously seen myself as different, even though my skin was five shades darker than everyone else's. I loved to play football like my friends, collect marbles like my friends and skip doing my homework, just like my friends.

But society has a funny way of dividing us humans into factions and tribes based on our bodies, politics and ideologies. We're separated by a fear of what isn't familiar and known. We become isolated, lonely and, in many cases, scared. This, in turn, causes more fear.

An antidote for fear

One of my favourite stories growing up and going to Buddhist school was the story of the Metta Sutta.

As the story goes, in the time of the historical Buddha, 500 monks were sent to the Himalayan forest to practise meditation. Back in those days, they believed devas (spirits) existed in the trees, plants and forest. As the monks settled and began their practice, the devas initially tolerated their presence. However, they soon came to realise that the monks wouldn't be leaving any time soon, so the devas made fearful sights and sounds at night to frighten them away.

Sure enough, the monks were spooked, their concentration was lost and many got sick. They decided to leave and return to the Buddha.

As my teacher translates it, upon their return the Buddha listened to the monks' complaints and pondered for a while, eventually responding, 'Bhikkus, I sent you out into the forest all on your own without any protection.' The monks listened on. 'Let me give you a weapon that you can take with you for protection.'

The Buddha sat them down and gave them the discourse of the Metta Sutta. The practice cultivates warmth, tenderness and kindness for ourselves as well as others. Armed with their weapon, the monks returned to the forest, practised loving kindness towards their surroundings and eventually became arahants (enlightened beings).

This story reminds us that we always have another way to respond to fear. We can open up to kindness, generosity and love. It's also a reminder that in trying times, a loving and gentle heart can be a potent weapon.

STILL TOGETHER

Absolute oneness is the belief that we are all one, that everything is connected. It's when we go beyond the mind, intellect and ego, or our ideas of who we think we are, and realise that my experience is largely similar to your experience. Within this also comes a realisation of our humanity – one that can be predicated on love and connection.

Relative oneness is different, however. Relative oneness is the sobering realisation that although we may all want love and connection, we are not one, not at this present moment. We do not have access to the resources that enable us to connect more deeply to these universal truths. We may be separated by our race, gender or sexual orientation. How can we be one if the world keeps telling us that we are not?

We may be drawn to the idea of oneness, but become frightened when we begin to understand the work we need to do in order to truly experience it. The reality is that we are all relatively different. We each have very different mindsets and experiences, with unique upbringings, support systems, skin colours and financial statuses. In order for us to be truly free, we must see how our freedom is dependent on the freedom of others. When we turn away from the reality of our experience – that oppression and suffering disproportionately affect certain people – we are informed by our biases and continue to strengthen them along with our world views. As a result, separation grows, and our sense of human connection shrinks.

At our best, humans recognise our humanity and are motivated to transform. At our worst, whether consciously or unconsciously, we don't care to. And when we don't care, we move away from a belief in common humanity and towards a belief in a divided world.

The invitation throughout this book is to examine our disconnections in a way that will help us feel more connected. To continuously see the ways in which we separate ourselves from others, out of fear or a lack of understanding. It's an invitation to remember our humanity, and our innate desire to feel connected to another human being. Remembering our humanity means cultivating empathy for all humans, even those who may cause us stress, pain or fear. Why? Because without the cultivation of these qualities towards all beings, oneness will only be conceptual. If we can't remind ourselves of our own humanity and our tendency to see what is negative, we miss out on seeing what is beautifully positive and has been there all along.

Some twenty years on from that day in school, I often think about those boys and their harsh words. I reflect on what they might have had to endure in their lives that led them to say what they said. Who taught them to think that way? It had to come from somewhere.

We all have the capacity to be those naive and innocent kids. In certain circumstances, we too may resort to harsh speech or action. When we look at each other in this way, we are able to recognise that we're all just responding to past conditioning and present causes. We each have within us the ability to harm another. We've done it before, and we will likely – knowingly or unknowingly – do it again. But we can also rest in the awareness that underneath, we are still basically good. Those boys wish to be happy in their lives too, and they too will feel the heartbreak of loss, sadness and suffering.

Even in moments when we feel the most 'othered', we still have the individual capacity to see humanity in each other. You are a good person, you don't have to do anything to prove it.

SELF-WORTH PRACTICE

**When you wake up, commit to reminding
yourself of your goodness.**

∞

You can do this before you go into a meeting or give
a presentation, before you walk out of home in
the morning or before you walk back in at the end
of the day.

Set a screensaver on your phone to remind you, or
simply reflect on this whenever it comes to your mind.

Think of the people you have helped in your
life and those who look forward to seeing you – this is
a reflection of your goodness.

Finally, remember that you don't have to do anything,
not even the previous four steps, to be worthy
of goodness. You are already good, you don't have
to prove it.

MINDFULNESS
(NOT STILLNESS)

∞

CHAPTER THREE

∞

Life can be crazy and beautiful,
can't it? As the Taoist sage Chuang Tzu
said 2000 years ago:

'When you open your heart,
you get life's ten thousand sorrows,
and ten thousand joys.'

It's inevitable that we will go through times when we are lost, confused and suffering, while at other times we will feel on top of the world and happy beyond our heart's capacity. Being human, chances are you won't be able to escape any of this. It's also what makes life such a poetic journey. If we can train our minds and hearts to be more open, compassionate and present, we can courageously meet all the challenges life throws at us with greater equanimity.

But the challenge for many of us is that we're often not fully engaged with our days, or our lives. We're at the mercy of our thoughts and emotions, susceptible to clever marketing and our own addictions. This is why a mindfulness practice can be very helpful – it can not only challenge but also change our perceptions, giving us more agency over how we're experiencing our lives. Mindfulness can alter the lens through which we see ourselves and, in turn, how we see the world around us.

Chapter Three

WELCOME TO THE WORLD OF MINDFULNESS

Chances are you have come across the term 'mindfulness' at some point in your life. This word has become part of the vernacular for many in the western world, and many attribute its popularity to Jon Kabat-Zinn, a professor of medicine at the University of Massachusetts Medical School. In 1979, he founded the university's Stress Reduction Clinic, where he initially ran tests on patients with chronic back pain, utilising practices and techniques he had learned from Buddhism. In stripping these practices of their Buddhist roots and branding them as part of a stress reduction program, he found that the patients' relationship to their pain changed. Some noticed that their emotional and mental stress had eased, and others even said their physical pain had lessened.

In the last 40-odd years, mindfulness practice has continued to penetrate mainstream society. From Eastern monasteries and retreat centres to celebrities and sportspeople, it's seeped into almost every aspect of our lives – think mindful parenting, mindful movement, mindful sex, mindful marketing, and so on. This explosion has largely come about as a result of research conducted over the last 40 years, which seems to show that practising mindfulness leads to significant improvements in one's brain and body. These include, but are not limited to, an ability to reduce stress, because we are better able to navigate stressful moments and cope. Through repeated practice, we can effectively shrink the amygdala, which is the stress centre of our body. Mindfulness has also been linked to an increased ability to regulate our emotions and improve our cognition and focus. Continued practice also has a positive effect on our immune system, making us less susceptible to illness. Perhaps most glaringly, mindfulness helps develop the psychological fortitude to be able to observe our thoughts instead of being at the mercy of them. In other words, we get to be the captain of our own ship more often.

Although the practice of mindfulness is readily accessible to many people these days, unfortunately it's not a panacea for life's problems. In fact, having a calm mind and being able to regulate our nervous system is only beneficial if we possess the wisdom to minimise our stresses in the first place.

MINDFULNESS BEYOND PRESENCE

Avoiding the discomfort of the present moment is what we humans do best. We crave the feeling of pleasure and ease. We'll often do anything to experience it and make it last; we'll deny reality or simply numb ourselves to it. Many of us have done this our whole life.

Finding ease doesn't have to involve eradicating our discomfort. We don't have to escape the present moment in order to move through it. Much of meditation practice is about confronting this unease, opening up our bodies and experiencing the challenges. We create space for feelings to arise and subside and notice how we identify the discomfort we feel as ours, and ours alone. Eventually, our practice teaches us to experience the joy and ease within the discomfort.

May this be a reminder: the tension you feel could be a good thing. Befriend it, ask it questions. It's there because you are getting closer to the truth.

Being present doesn't
mean feeling good.

Resting in a compassionate presence is a beautiful and wondrous thing. If all we do throughout our lives is remain present and kind to those around us, this is an achievement in itself. But, for many, this may not be enough. If we are constantly battling our own minds and observe negative behavioural patterns, we may want to look a little deeper.

Before I dived deeper into Buddhist meditation practice with my teachers, I was largely practising unguided on my own, save for a few instructions from my first teacher. At that point, I was aware of my anxiety and my stress. Throughout the day, I noticed how my heart would race or my palms would start sweating – but it didn't go away because I noticed it. I was compassionate towards my addictions – I knew that I was consuming because I was in pain – but they also stayed with me. I was yanked around by my thoughts and emotions, and even though I had moments of peace, the confusion and anxiety eventually returned, bringing with it more judgement and guilt and shame.

The day my life began to really transform was when my practice asked me to look at the root causes of these issues. I had to stop meditating when I was in pain and look at what was causing my pain. Was it my lifestyle? What was I chasing? What did I value? How was I in relation to others? How was I eating, and what mattered to me at that point? I had to create space to feel my suffering.

Answering such questions, I knew, would lead me to the heart of the matter. In order to do this, I had to develop the quality of insight, cultivating an analytical mind towards my behaviour and my unconscious tendencies. When we go beyond presence, we move towards this level of understanding of our mind.

When people talk about what lies beyond mindfulness as most people know it, my answer is simple: Buddhist mindfulness. This path doesn't consider mindfulness meditation as simply a technique to reach a doorway to happiness, but as a doorway to another door. The path can be long and arduous but ultimately offers us the freedom and happiness we seek. It considers mindfulness as a key component of one's happiness, but not the sole path. It involves the Buddha's foundational teachings called the Four Noble Truths.

The Buddhist path drew me in because I knew I didn't want to suffer the way that I was anymore. It was also the only practice that bluntly told me that I was largely responsible for the majority of my suffering. My teacher was right – I had the tools I needed to feel more engaged with my life. They had been with me all along.

The Four Noble Truths

In life there is suffering

Suffering can sound like a heavy word for some. We may have a picture of suffering as being a significant life event that causes us pain. While that may be true, what the Buddha is talking about here can also be understood as unsatisfactoriness. Whether we are conscious of it or not, we go through our life experiencing a lot of it – physically, mentally or emotionally. We experience it when we don't get what we want. We also experience it when we do get what we want. We also come to realise that there is a quality of impermanence to so much of our life and this in turn also causes us to suffer because we inevitably want things to be permanent. We want love to last. We want our family and friends to live forever and we want our bodies to never lose their shape. But all of this is subject to change and, you guessed it, this makes us suffer.

The principal cause of this suffering is our clinging

Think for a moment about these words: attachment, craving, desiring, holding on, addicted, obsessed and thirsty. They all have a sense of suffering contained within them. We can cling or become attached to our views on things, our loved ones, pleasurable experiences and a fixed sense of self. We can cling to the way things ought to be instead of how they really are. Waking up to the first noble truth is acknowledging the many ways we crave and desire for life and the present moment to be different to the way it actually is.

We can end our suffering

The end of suffering is the end of clinging. Here we learn that there is a way for us not to suffer (relatively) in our life. We have to let go of our clinging. This is easier said than done, but what we're really talking about is being mindful of the ways we cling and identify with our experiences. From here we can make decisions that lead us towards happiness instead of suffering. This may mean being open to new ways of doing things or thinking, letting go of a grudge or simply choosing to observe a strong emotion instead of reacting.

Here is how we do it; the eightfold path

The Buddha outlines a pathway for us to practise cultivating our hearts and minds towards happiness and equanimity. These aren't the Ten Commandments; they're more of an invitation to explore this path for yourself and see if it alleviates stress and worry in your life.

1. Right understanding (Samma ditthi)
This means understanding reality as reality. Simply put, this is understanding the four noble truths.

2. Right thought (Samma sankappa)
We can practise meditation and mindfulness in a way that will shape our thoughts towards love, kindness and harmony, and away from greed, hatred, ill-will and violence.

3. Right speech (Samma vaca)
Not telling lies and speaking harshly about people, and definitely not causing hate or unrest among people.

4. Right action (Samma kammanta)

That we don't do anything that causes harm or destruction. We practise being moral and peaceful and non-violent towards ourselves or others through our actions.

5. Right livelihood (Samma ajiva)

Simply put, we make a living that does not cause harm to others.

6. Right effort (Samma vayama)

This is the work we put in to cultivating a mind and life that does not harm, and that cultivates wholesome states to arise.

7. Right mindfulness (Samma sati)

Here we remain mindful of our body, feelings, mind and mental processes.

8. Right concentration (Samma samadhi)

Concentration comes to us through our effort, mindfulness and application. It is the doorway to cultivating a mindful life through a focused and aware mind.

STILL TOGETHER

Where mindfulness all began

Originally brought to the world through the teachings of the Satipatthana Sutta in the Theravada Buddhist tradition, mindfulness is a foundational practice of cultivating awareness, equanimity and mindful conduct. We do this in the hope that we may live our lives with greater happiness and less dissatisfaction.

Traditionally, this was known as the elimination of greed, hatred and delusion.

Although many of us may have heard of the word mindfulness and perhaps practise it already, the traditional teachings tell us that it's more than simply paying attention to the moment-by-moment experience. Sure, we begin there, but the teachings tell us that we can in fact use the practice to go beneath the surface of our everyday experiences, which tend to be shrouded with projections, emotions and habitual thinking. When we go beyond the present moment and cultivate our minds to become more aware, we can see things as they really are, which is what lies at the heart of this path. When we see things as they really are, we're able to move through our lives with less suffering, greater equanimity and, ultimately, more happiness. We have an understanding of which thoughts and actions lead us towards this happiness and which thoughts and actions lead us in the opposite direction. Ultimately, we know we are (mostly) in control

Papañca

Now more than ever, notice the present moment,
and the stories you tell yourself about it.

The mind has a funny way of taking us on trips to weird
and wonderful places, usually without telling us. Ever
made up a story about someone on Instagram whom
you've never met? Or created a narrative around someone
who looked at you in a weird way?

In Buddhist meditation practice, we call this papañca.
An endless movie of all the things that never happened.
This happens to me all the time when I'm on silent retreat
and I create a story about that one guy who goes back for
seconds at lunch, for example. However, this also afflicts
us in everyday life. In moments where we may be resting,
rejuvenating or tending to our sadness, we can feel the
pangs of our own judgement and shame.

Mindfulness practice is about cutting through these
false perceptions and seeing things as they are. It's about
embracing the transience of our thoughts as simply
thoughts and not an innate reflection of our value.

STILL TOGETHER

'Only in the reality of
the present can we love,
can we awaken, can we find
peace and understanding
and connection with
ourselves and the world.'

Jack Kornfield

of how we respond to life. This practice isn't always easy, but with sincere effort and diligent practice, we develop our mind and heart muscles in a way that gives us more agency in our lives.

At the beginning of this journey, we start to set ourselves a baseline of presence and awareness for us to explore the deeper truths of our lives. For example, we don't need to be Buddhist to know that the more attentive we can be towards our loved ones when they are going through a hard time, the more love and connection we can create. Or, when we are immersed in the presence of simple, everyday activities like walking in the park, we may be filled with a spontaneous burst of gratitude and connection. Deep presence brings with it a realisation that in this very moment, things are how they are. Sure, we might have loan repayments piling up, our relationships might be rocky – hell, we may even find ourselves in the middle of a global pandemic – but if you're reading these words, at this very moment, you're okay. This is presence.

The good news is that many of us are already mindful.

There's a host of everyday activities to which we already apply what I call basic mindfulness. Can you remember the last deep and meaningful conversation you had with someone? The connection you felt during and afterwards? Do you recall what it's like to cook a meal, and feel your senses come alive with the aromas and texture of the produce? Or perhaps it was at work during a high-pressure period where you felt yourself completely immersed in your task, in a flow state.

But inevitably, things change. Whether it's a job or a relationship or an exercise routine, the novelty of the 'new' wears off and the spark is gone , and along with it our sense of being in the moment. We each have the power, however, to bring some magic back into our day-to-day lives, even when nothing particularly thrilling is happening.

If we can commit to living mindfully and choose to engage our curiosity and be tender towards ourselves and others, we're able to be present to the changing beauty in all things without clinging to fixed views about how things should be. We learn to be emotionally flexible and to be open to the momentary experience. From this place, we fine tune our ability to witness our minds at work instead of being at their whim, and we begin to see things with much more clarity.

Seeing things clearly is a fundamental goal of mindfulness. Many of us are navigating lives that are stressful or relationships that are complex, or are simply feeling busy or lonely, or sometimes both. When our minds are unsettled and we are not engaged with the present moment, our perceptions of the world are altered. Being aware of ourselves and our bearings and not projecting our feelings onto others is a superpower.

In Pali, the language of the Buddha, the word for mindfulness is 'sati'. Translated, it means 'to remember'. Remembering is simply awareness combined with the wisdom in the way things are.

When we bring awareness to our thoughts and actions, we can see the feelings and perceptions that give rise to them. In doing so, we cultivate understanding of why we do what we do, which goes beyond simply noticing what we do. Why do certain patterns follow us throughout our lives? Why do we end up in similar relationships? Or work situations that feel familiar? This kind of awareness invites us to thoroughly engage with our lives, to not only be present but to also reflect on whether our actions in the world are truly helpful. But are our actions kind, generous and thoughtful? Or are they greedy, or coming from a place of anger or confusion?

The more we become aware of these things, the more we see that when we act out of anger or hatred, this leads to more stress or anxiety and ultimately doesn't feel very good. . But when we choose to act out of empathy, awareness and compassion, this makes us feel tangibly better.

The way to check in on this is through meditation, but the Buddha also taught us that we should practise mindfulness at all times. Whether we're talking, eating or lying down, every moment presents an opportunity to practise mindfulness and, more importantly, to see reality. This is where mindfulness in this capacity goes beyond just presence and cultivates a wisdom in our awareness. We clear the filters through which we see the world and reduce any harm we may cause, even unwittingly. But this takes practice and dedication. When we choose the path of clear seeing, we open ourselves up to reality in all its beauty and chaos.

CHECK-IN

∞

Check in with your body and ask yourself,
does it feel good to yell at someone?
Does it feel good to lie to someone?

Then check in next time you help someone
or show kindness towards another, and notice
the difference.

THE FOUR FOUNDATIONS OF MINDFULNESS

The body

Let's start our exploration here. This may sound obvious, but we'll often be surprised about how little time we spend being present to our bodies. The body is a fertile ground for observation and if we observe it with mindfulness, this will serve us well. Doing this is also the easiest and quickest way for us to cultivate the quality of presence. When we're paying attention to the subtleties of the body we're spending less time lost in our thoughts. Being in our bodies is foundational to everything that follows. If we're not here, we're not present. For many of us, this first stage can be a revelation in itself. That's why a preliminary mindfulness practice involves becoming fully aware of our bodies.

The most obvious point of focus in your body is your breath, which is the basis of all four of the foundations. Breathing occurs without any control or manipulation, and it is literally the thing keeping you alive. Sometimes its focal point is clear and perceptible at the tip of our nose; at other times it's evident in our stomach or, when we're exercising hard or feeling anxious, in our chest. Allowing our minds to rest on where our breath is anchored (belly, nose, chest) has a calming effect on the nervous system. Not only is our body and our breath an anchor for our minds, it's also communicating with us moment by moment, telling us how we feel. It might be the quickening of our breath due to anxiety, or perhaps due to the butterflies we feel when we meet someone special.

If we pay closer attention to our bodies, we can listen to the messages that it's constantly sending our way. What do our tight shoulders tell us about our current state? Or our constant migraines when we're talking to a colleague? Deeper yet, why is there a feeling of sadness in your stomach, or a feeling of grief near your chest? We often don't recognise these subtle cues – instead, we try to bypass these feelings by numbing ourselves. If we're attentive and non-judgemental, our bodies can teach us a great deal.

BODY SCAN MEDITATION

A simple body scan meditation during which we notice sensations in various parts of our body brings awareness to those parts of our body, which we may not have been aware of. In the process, our mind calms down as our brain focuses on this one thing.

∞

As you begin to pay attention to your different body parts, you may start to become aware of processes that usually go unnoticed.

Your heart is beating, pumping blood into your muscles. Oxygen is being transported around your body, and day by day you are changing and evolving.

Feelings

As we begin to pay attention to our body, we soon notice something really interesting: feelings begin to arise. This might be the feeling of discomfort, or the feeling of frustration because we think we're not 'doing it right'. This may lead to deeper feelings of anger and resentment, and perhaps even shame and self-loathing. But underneath these labelled emotions is a primary feeling tone: either pleasant, unpleasant or neutral. We experience one of these feeling tones due to a multitude of reasons, simply as a result of being human. But identifying the tone of the feeling, rather than focusing on the feeling itself, helps us to avoid getting lost in the story of the feeling. Becoming mindful of our feelings can help us to tolerate and sit with unpleasant feelings as we acknowledge and validate them. Eventually, if we learn not to react to them, they begin to dissipate, because feelings, like all things, are impermanent.

Mind or attitudes

As we keep observing the body and notice feelings arise, attitudes or mind states may begin to form. We may pursue or crave pleasant feelings due to the desire to always feel good, and to avoid negative feelings at all costs. But life is full of undesirable moments, from being stuck in traffic to having to listen to a racist uncle at Christmas or a boss who triggers you. Here, our mindfulness practice becomes a real tool for noticing how we react when we are experiencing an unhelpful state such as anger. Ever said something you regretted straight away? Me too. When we're aware of our mind states, we can more readily unhook from that feeling tone because we know how it's going to end – usually, not well. We can learn to observe our mental states without judgement and watch them come and go, rather than reacting to them. We start to understand how our minds are like the sky. Our thoughts, ideas and feelings are essentially like clouds drifting in and out, all of which interrupt our ability to be present with our bodies.

Here we learn about the five hindrances, or primary roadblocks, that keep us lost in our thoughts.

The five hindrances

Sensory desire

These are simply desires of the senses. If we hear
the voice of someone we know, we may get lost in
a desire to see them. Or if we smell something tasty,
our senses rapidly shift towards trying to acquire
the object producing the smell.

Ill will

This is when we may be feeling anger or resentment
towards ourselves or others. This can often feel
quite strong and take our mind and body away from
our awareness as we get lost in our rage.

Anxiety

This occurs when our minds simply can't be still.
They are jumping around from one thought to another,
like a monkey jumping from branch to branch.

Sloth and torpor

I always loved this one. Firstly, because it sounds
hilarious, and secondly, because it sums up how many
of us arrive on the cushion. Sloth and torpor refer to
our inability to sustain an energy for our practice due
to a layer of laziness. Procrastination is another way this
hindrance shows up, and it can be very cleverly disguised
as perfectionism. Both serve to keep us away from
showing up for our practice.

Doubt

I have perhaps experienced doubt more than any other
hindrance. This is when you feel like you're just not doing
it right. You're unsure if your practice is working or if
you're even capable of meditating. Basically, you doubt
the whole practice and wonder if you should just take
up Pilates. This is where it's best to connect with a wise
teacher or a community of meditators.

Mental processes

This aspect of the practice really encapsulates all of the first three foundations, or stages, and can be understood as awareness of awareness itself. My dear friend and wise teacher Anu Gupta gave me this great example: 'So, imagine you become aware of the mind wanting something ... fame, money, power, whatever the story is. Well, we can be aware of the hindrances in that story (desire, aversion, etc.), we can be aware of the feeling tone, we can be aware of the sensations in the body – but, ultimately, we can become aware of the awareness that is aware of all of those things simultaneously. And then we let it all go.'

We become aware of what's occurring by developing awareness through the body, then we notice our body's feeling tones: like, dislike, neutral. With this information, we develop an attitude or a state of mind attached to the feeling. We may crave or avoid elements of our life or our experience. What stories have we created, what narratives have we formed and what 'world' have we created in our minds?

How are we unconsciously trying to manipulate situations or control things? This is where we begin to deepen the act of seeing things 'as they are'. We see both the impermanence and, importantly, the interconnection of all things. Everything we experience as 'mine' – my anxiety, my grief, my shame, my pain – causes and conditions, and is not a reflection of who we are. Mindfulness helps us to see that these experiences don't belong to us. They are simply influenced by these causes and conditions. This realisation allows us to let go, to be equanimous with our current state and engage with our life with confidence.

These stages don't have to be practised individually. You can experience them all in a single sitting, or simply observe them in daily life. It all starts with the simple first step of noticing our breath and our bodies.

The foundations of mindfulness help us to identify the various states and stories we tell ourselves and show us how to unhook from them. They give us the potential to respond to our thoughts, emotions and stories more wisely, ultimately untangling us from negative states and creating the conditions for happiness.

Austrian neurologist, psychiatrist and author Viktor Frankl gifted us with these words of wisdom:

> 'Between stimulus and response there is a space.
> In that space is our power to choose our response.
> In our response lies our growth and our freedom.'

Frankl is speaking about mindfulness. This is the space between our conditioned responses, our unmet needs and our emotions, and our response, which can come from a place of awareness and move us towards clarity and wisdom.

START WHERE
YOU ARE

∞

CHAPTER FOUR

∞

For many, the path to meditation might seem arduous or complex. But it need not be. It won't take much for you to begin seeing the benefits of a regular mindfulness practice. Really, all you need is a genuine intention to be more present and kind towards yourself and the world around you.

BEGINNER'S MIND

In practice, beginner's mind invites us to be open to possibilities. Whatever arises, be it difficult or satisfying, is an opportunity to learn and grow. And through practising this way we begin to see how our fixed views about ourselves and the world around us actually impede our growth.

As beginners, we fiddle and fumble our way through the learning, making mistakes along the way as we navigate new material. This doesn't make us bad students or people; it makes us human. The contemplation is what these instructions can teach us about navigating the present moment and our own fixed view of the world.

The subtle art of non-knowing

Much of meditation practice can be about learning what it means to not-know. We will often oscillate between moments of happiness and peace and moments of anxiety and pain. We sign up for this when we are born. This is being human. With mindfulness, we give ourselves more opportunities to soften into life's uncertainties. Not knowing how things will go or what we're feeling, or even being unsure of what step to take next, offers us an opportunity to soften.

When we're feeling groundless, we're conditioned to cling to things that make us feel safe.

However, life is inherently groundless and always was. It is always unstable and uncertain, no matter how long you might feel like it isn't. When we rest and soften into this feeling of not-knowing, what comes up is a letting go and an air of spaciousness. Spaciousness is what I tell people true love feels like. Spaciousness doesn't demand or judge. Spaciousness liberates us.

'In the beginner's mind there are many possibilities, but in the expert's there are few.'

– Suzuki Roshi

STILL TOGETHER

MEDITATION

It can be hugely beneficial to deepen your mindfulness practice through meditation. There are some basic instructions in this book, or you can connect with a teacher and, over time, a community of meditators. I'll tell you why this is important later.

My meditation teacher's first instructions to me were:

'Sit down, close your eyes and notice what comes up.'

They were fairly loose instructions, and, admittedly, my practice was very interesting during those first six months. I was certain that my mind was too busy, I had too many thoughts and I was defective in some way – and that meditation just wouldn't work for me. Thankfully, I later realised I wasn't the only person in the world who had thoughts during meditation. The more I practised, the more I understood the meaning behind those instructions and was able to study them with my teacher in greater depth. These days, meditation instructions are a bit more detailed, and we also have access to mobile meditation apps, YouTube videos and an abundance of incredible teachers all over the world.

Meditation practice is simple, but it's not easy. There will be many ups and downs in your practice. Much like me in those first six months, there will be times when you will probably want to quit. You will likely be uncomfortable, both physically and mentally.

You may cry, you may get angry, you may tell yourself (and anyone else you speak to) that meditation is simply not for you and you're going to stick to Pilates instead.

I want to remind you that this is normal. I experienced all of these thought patterns, just as I'm sure the millions of other people who meditate daily also do. If this practice was easy, it simply wouldn't be so profound. When we sit down to calm our minds and open our hearts, we are working against a lifetime of distraction and poor habits. The difference is, we are finally seeing it clearly, and this should be celebrated. Given that many of us have never been taught how to relate to our thoughts, it's no wonder that our experience may be challenging at first. Anything new will challenge us and take us outside of our comfort zone. Such is life – it is not suitably pleasant 24 hours a day.

One thing that we must do at some point in our life is endure moments that are difficult. If we refuse to do this in our life, we will simply be practising aversion – avoiding moments that may turn out to be monumental. Some of life's most joyful moments come from moments of challenge – childbirth, achieving a goal, getting a promotion at work – all wrapped up in moments of discomfort.

The good news is that our meditation practice teaches us how to sit with the pleasant and the unpleasant. Not only to navigate the discomfort when we're practising, but also when we're out in the world. If we can sit and notice that our minds are wandering and simply and non-judgementally bring our attention back to the breath or a sound, then we can sit with the fear and doubt of public speaking. If we can turn towards our anger or sadness in our meditation practice with a warm and compassionate response, then we can be there for ourselves and others in periods of loss and grief.

Our meditation practice is simply a reflection of our life. How we relate to our thoughts and our breath is how we relate to everything in our life.

The following is what I suggest for students looking to create a new, sustainable meditation practice.

'Meditation for me is practice
for when the sh*t really hits
the fan. Sometimes we can
over-emphasize the present
moment idea of meditation but
it's really building your capacity
to hold more, whether that's
this week or in two years
when something shows up
that you didn't necessarily
plan for or want.'

Sebene Selassie

STILL TOGETHER

HOW TO PREPARE FOR YOUR MEDITATION

Find a motivation

Firstly, ask yourself why you want to meditate. What is your motivation? This is an important part of our preparation as we reflect on what will motivate us to get up out of bed each day, what will drive us to sit when we're sad or unhappy, what will be the petrol to our engine that moves us forward, especially when we don't want to move. I ask my students to get really clear with this. Not only will it motivate us to meditate, but it will also inform what sort of meditation we practise. Do we want to sleep better? Stress less? Or do we want to feel more connected to others or heal our emotional wounds? Perhaps you could consider that your practice is actually not about you at all. It's for the benefit of those closest to you – your kids, your partner, your community. Humanity itself can benefit from you having a calmer and wiser mind and a more generous and empathetic heart. I find that a motivation involving benefits for others is far more potent than one that only concerns ourselves. But I invite you to explore this for yourself, knowing that as your practice grows, so too will your motivation. You can think big, but start small.

Find a comfortable and reliable place to practise

We may not all have a beautifully decorated meditation cove in our home. But it doesn't matter if you live in a share house or are surrounded by kids' toys, we can all find a meditation space to call our own. When I first began, I simply sat up straight on my bed with a candle lit in front of me. I had noisy housemates, but it was all I could do at the time. Just do the best that you can. I suggest choosing a location that feels calming, ideally somewhere you can light a candle or put up some photos of people you're inspired by – maybe your family or someone you look up to. This is not because you are praying to them, it's as a reminder of their goodness and the admiration and care you feel for them. You might call upon the energy of a teacher before you start, to help you navigate your practice, or even your dog. A simple but meaningful set-up creates a ritual where you go to honour yourself and the present moment by turning inward.

Set realistic expectations

One of the quickest ways to kill your practice is to create unrealistic expectations. Kudos to you if you manage to have a blissful experience in meditation every time. I'm not one of those people, and neither are many of the millions of people who practice meditation daily. Meditation is a skill, and when learning any new skill there will be bumps and roadblocks along the way. Be gentle with yourself and know that the practice works best when it's done over time, consistently.

Choose your practice and set a reasonable time

With the wonderful amount of choice we have these days, there are literally thousands of meditations we can practise at any given time. This is both good and bad. I'm of the belief that practising under a particular stream or lineage is the best way to experience depth. If we're jumping around from practice to practice, how will we know if we're gaining insight? I suggest starting with mindful practices such as a body scan or shamata (see the instructions on the following pages), or even loving kindness practice. All of these practices create meditative awareness, develop concentration and foster compassion. When it comes to the duration of your meditation, think big, but start small. Five to ten minutes every day is a lot more useful than 20 minutes once a week.

Get comfortable – but not too comfortable

Being at ease in your meditation posture is vital, otherwise all you will be thinking about in practice is how uncomfortable you are.

1. When you begin you can sit on a chair, couch, bed or, if you're open to doing so, on some cushions in front of your makeshift altar. Prop up your sitz bones by elevating your hips so they are above your knees. Make sure your knees aren't higher than your hips – trust me, it ain't pleasant.

2. Make sure your spine is relatively straight, so your body is upright and alert without being too rigid or forced.

3. Try not to arch your neck up or down. Instead, imagine you are staring into the eyes of your favourite person, who is sitting right in front of you.

4. Keep your lips closed, your teeth gently apart, and the tip of your tongue against the back of your upper teeth.

5. You can keep your eyes open, but I suggest starting with eyes closed – this helps keep us from being too distracted.

6. Then, soften into your body, reminding yourself of its presence and current goal – to be fully aware, in this moment.

Once you've prepared adequately, the next step is to choose the type of meditation that aligns with your motivation. If your motivation is to feel less stressed and calmer, you may want a meditation that both relaxes your body and calms your mind. I suggest starting with one of the two practices outlined on the following pages. A sounds and body scan meditation, or a shamata (calm abiding) meditation.

SOUNDS AND BODY SCAN MEDITATION

This is a fantastic practice for those new to meditation or those of us with an overactive mind. The idea of this particular meditation is to bring gentle awareness to different sensory objects.

∞

1. Once you've gone through the preparations
for meditation, start to bring your awareness to
the sounds around you.

2. You don't have to analyse what these sounds are or
where they come from, simply notice sounds as sounds.

3. Now bring your awareness to the sounds that are
the most obvious. This might be the sound of traffic or
people walking or talking outside. Without identifying
what the sound is, simply notice this obvious sound.

4. Then notice the sounds that are less obvious
and subtle.

5. Notice where they are coming from.

6. Then begin to shift your awareness to the feeling of
your feet. Observe the feet through your sense of touch.
Do you notice a warmth or tingling feeling?

7. Notice your legs, effortlessly. Observe the feeling of your legs – front and back, upper and lower, in no particular order.

8. Notice your buttocks, your back, your arms and your hands.

9. Observe the front of your body, your chest, your stomach and your face.

10. Stay with the observation of your body, noticing the different parts all working together as one.

You might get lost after the first instruction, but guess what? That's actually quite normal. What makes this mindfulness practice mindful is our ability to recognise that our mind has wandered away. Knowing that our mind has wandered away is an accomplishment of our mind! It's not proof that we're useless. When we recognise that this has happened, and bring awareness back to the body or sound with warmth and tenderness, we're being mindful.

STILL TOGETHER

SHAMATA (CALM ABIDING) MEDITATION

Shamata meditation is commonly known as mindfulness meditation. It's a systematic way to cultivate a calm and peaceful mind. In shamata practice, we can use any number of supports (or anchors) for our mind to focus on. Here we will use the breath, but eventually we want to get to a place where we don't use any supports and simply rest naturally in awareness. The breath acts as a bridge for our awareness to deepen.

∞

1. Once you've gone through the preparations
for meditation, start to bring a gentle awareness
to your body. Take a few moments to settle into your
body and notice if there are any predominant
feelings coming up.

2. Bring your awareness to your breath, wherever it is
the most obvious to you. This could be in your stomach,
or at the tip of your nose.

3. Try not to change or force your breath at this point.
We don't want to manipulate the breath in any way,
we're simply trying to bring awareness to something that
we don't usually pay much attention to. You can label
the end of each out breath using the word 'out'.

4. As you rest, thoughts and ideas will arise and throw
you off. Each time they do, silently say to yourself
'thinking' and then return to your breath.

5. After a few moments, the mind will again begin to wander. Again, calmly respond with 'thinking' and return to the breath. There is no story and no judgement.

6. Over and over again, we continue with this basic, but not easy, process.

As you deepen your shamata practice, you'll notice how wildly active your mind naturally is. Again, this is a good thing. We finally see clearly that our minds are thinking at a million miles per hour. Now we have the ability to train our mind to calm down and thereby respond better and more wisely to our thoughts.

Mindfulness of the moments we are not mindful ... is mindfulness.

Even mindfulness is impermanent. Remembering the impermanence of mindfulness is the very practice of mindfulness. How sobering this is for all of us, eh? The more we see how fleeting our awareness is — the deeper we get in touch with it. Understanding this is the beginning to seeing reality as reality.

STILL TOGETHER

MINDFULNESS
IN DAILY LIFE

∞

CHAPTER FIVE

∞

Bringing mindfulness and meditation practice
into our lives through foundational practices
can transform us from the inside out.
Our ability to respond to stress will grow,
and our decision-making and levels of focus
will also improve. But perhaps the most potent
aspect of a regular mindfulness practice is how
it allows us to interact with the world around
us. It's all good and well to sit in a quiet place
and meditate for 20 minutes a day, but it's
useless if the quality of our lives and of those
around us isn't improving during the remaining
23 hours and 40 minutes.

BRINGING MINDFULNESS TO LIFE

Perhaps there is no greater place where we are challenged in our daily lives than in our relationships with others. It is usually the people around that trigger the most stress and anxiety. These people are also the ones that point out what we can't see and where we have room to grow. Thankfully, they are also the ones that see the effects of our mindfulness practice first and validate that what we're doing is working.

In this chapter we'll explore different aspects of our lives that may benefit from mindfulness practice.

MINDFULNESS
IN LOVE

Here's what I know to be true. Falling in love is easy. Staying in love, that's the real work.

I'm sure flying a plane is difficult, but with proper training and study and enough logged hours, you could probably make a fine pilot one day. Similarly, learning to cook can be tricky, but if you practise enough, you're bound to eventually make something reasonably edible. But who teaches us how to love? It's not on the high school curriculum and there are no tutors I'm aware of who teach humans how to function optimally in a relationship. Being in a relationship is hard work.

For many of us, our ideas of love and relationships are formed from a young age, based on what we observe in our environment – namely, the behaviours of our parents or guardians – as well as what we read in novels and see in movies. And if you're anything like me, your early childhood memories were complex, maybe even traumatic. We hear people around us talk about their feelings, emotions, hopes and dreams and we start to hope that we too might experience something similar. Our ideas mix with our delusions and we dream of an ideal relationship with an ideal partner. This idea of the perfect partner is something that many of us find hard to shake.

'I want to be in a
relationship where you
telling me you love me
is just a ceremonious
validation of what you
already show me.'

– Steve Maraboli

It's no wonder so many relationships fail after the honeymoon period. We tell ourselves that we have fallen out of love. We go from texting daily to avoiding their calls, from declarations of love to asking them to pick up milk on the way home. What once turned us on about our partners suddenly annoys us beyond belief.

But the honeymoon period of any relationship is purely a heightened state of mindfulness. Mindfulness is our capacity to be in the present moment with a sense of curiosity and compassion. In the honeymoon period, you start off wanting to spend as much time with your partner as possible. You're hungry to learn more about them: 'What's your favourite colour?' 'What movie made you cry recently?' 'How did you get that scar?' You wait for their answers and you listen attentively. If something slightly annoying happens – perhaps they forgot it's date night or they misplaced their car keys – you laugh it off. You're genuinely interested in your partner, and you're patient and compassionate towards them.

Mindfulness is the basic human ability to be fully present, to be aware of where we are and what we're doing, and not to be overly reactive to or overwhelmed by what's going on around us. It's not some woo-woo that you have to spend hours researching or travel to a faraway land to find. It's available to you and your partner right now.

So how can living a more mindful life help you cultivate a greater relationship?

Your first relationship is with yourself

'Your relationship to yourself is and always will be directly reflected in all your relationships with others.'

– Vironika Tugaleva

Firstly, ask yourself, am I in this relationship because I'm scared to be alone? In many spiritual texts, the first teachings are about the nature of our most important relationship – the one we have with ourselves. We are asked to listen, to be patient and to understand our own thoughts and tendencies so we can find compassion for the parts of ourselves we might not like so much. Loneliness, anger, fear, jealousy – they tend to exist in all of us. Some of us have a handle on this, while others don't. Having a truly meaningful relationship depends on our capacity to be alone and okay with ourselves. A mindful person recognises when they are clinging to their partner out of a sense of lack. We can then detach from this unhealthy thought and develop more clarity through awareness of our tendencies. We can't change what we can't see, so becoming more self-aware is vitally important.

Be present

'If you love someone, the greatest gift
you can give them is your presence.'

– Thich Nhat Hanh

This is a no-brainer. How can we relate to ourselves and our partners if we are not even there? And you know what I'm talking about, Susan. Scrolling through Snapchat while your partner asks about your day, or watching the football when your partner asks you for the third time to take the rubbish out – that's not being present. It's being absent. Relationships can't flourish with absence. Resolve to put your phones down when you go out to dinner, and spend a designated time, morning or night (or both!), being fully present to your partner.

Listen, for no other reason than to listen

'Most people do not listen with the intent to understand;
they listen with the intent to reply.'

– Stephen R Covey

We are hard-wired to look for problems. To fix things.
But sometimes we don't need someone to fix our problems; we
just need someone to hear them. Listening to our partner is a
powerful exercise in presence and love. When we listen, we open
up our capacity to understand. And truly meaningful relationships
prosper when we understand each other – our hopes, our fears,
our stresses and our triggers. When we listen deeply, we can see
not only what our partner is communicating through their words,
but also through their eyes and body. Mindful listening opens us
up to a much deeper level of connection.

Have compassion

'Too often we underestimate the power of a touch, a smile,
a kind word, a listening ear, an honest compliment, or the
smallest act of caring, all of which have the potential
to turn a life around.'

– Leo Buscaglia

Compassion, or 'karuna' in the Pali language, is the capacity each
of us has not only to empathise with another person, but also
to genuinely help them suffer less. It's born out of listening and
understanding. It's our capacity to help our partner hurt less after
a long day at work or after something has gone wrong. It's also
our capacity to understand that they are a human, not just a body
that you co-exist with. A human who experiences fear, hope,
anxiety and a sense of being overwhelmed, just like you do.
Seeing your partner as a human can dramatically change the
nature of a relationship, because it means we see in them what
we have in us: an imperfectly perfect human trying to do the
best they can with what they have. Our partner is also someone
who makes mistakes when they are scared, confused or tired.
Through this lens of compassion, we can better understand
ourselves and each other.

Remember that this too shall pass

'Life's impermanence, I realised, is what makes every single day so precious. It's what shapes our time here. It's what makes it so important that not a single moment be wasted.'

– Wes Moore

Far from looking at impermanence as a gloomy topic, it can actually be quite liberating. This has been the most transformative practice for me in my relationship. Knowing that our time with our partner is in one way or another limited means we don't always get caught up in the little stresses of life, such as petty arguments over the toilet seat being left up or the fact that she's always buying new cushions. Accepting that our time together will eventually come to an end gives us the freedom to experience our days and our partner with a sense of genuine love and gratitude.

The reality is, all our time is limited. We can choose to spend it caught up in our mind or we can choose to live a life filled with what really matters.

A mindful life allows us to be fully present to what surrounds us, the people and the experiences, while we manage the ups and downs of life with a genuine sense of calm, compassion and clarity.

MINDFULNESS IN FRIENDSHIPS

Kalyāṇa-mitta – Spiritual friendship

If bringing mindfulness into our relationships is one of the most challenging aspects of our life, then bringing mindfulness into our friendships might be the most important one.

In romantic relationships, we're often heavily emotionally invested. When it comes to our family members, our childhood experiences and psychology cloud our ability to see each member in a completely open and unbiased way. But friendship is different – it's always a choice. We choose our friends, and they choose us. With our close friends, we can drift away and come together and have it feel like no time has passed. These friendships also allow for a certain level of transparency that we don't usually experience with our parents or lovers. Our truly close friends see us at our worst and at our best, and accept all of it. More often than not, they can see us more clearly than we can see ourselves.

When the Buddha was asked by one of his students, Ananda, if friendship was part of one's spiritual path, the Buddha quickly replied, 'No, Ananda, friendship is the entire path.'

We may think of meditation and spiritual practice as a lonely, isolated experience. After all, one closes one's eyes and simply

Not beating yourself up – a love story

It's a beautifully human aspect of our lives that we can make mistakes, learn from them and then show up for ourselves and our loved ones in more powerful ways. However, we often attach a painful narrative to the mistakes we have made in the past that keeps us trapped in a cycle of guilt and shame.

It's important that we acknowledge the impact of our actions towards ourselves and others but also be willing to acknowledge our state of awareness at the time. Eventually there will come a time when we must commit to not making the same mistakes again and move forward with our precious human life.

We stay trapped in suffering if we take on the belief that our mistakes are who we are at our core, instead of a moment in time in which we lacked clarity or wisdom. Mistakes can form a powerful springboard that launches us in the direction of living a compassionate and virtuous life – one that begins with a deep love for our own humanity.

'In everyone there is the
capacity to wake up,
to understand, and to love.'

– Thich Nhat Hanh

observes one's actions and experiences, over and over and over again. It's not exactly a social activity. But our spiritual practice isn't one in which we separate ourselves from others or the world, it's one where we can engage with the world more fully. And this is why friendship is so important along our journey.

Meghiya, a student and attendant of the Buddha, once asked him if he could take his leave from watching over Buddha and meditate under a mango grove he saw on one of his daily walks.

'We're alone, Meghiya, wait till another monk returns,' said the Buddha.

Meghiya protested. 'Buddha, you have nothing more to do, and nothing that needs improvement. But I have. If you allow me, I'd like to go back to that mango grove to meditate.'

'We're alone, Meghiya, wait till another monk returns,' responded the Buddha.

Meghiya tried again.

'But, Buddha, you have nothing more to do, and nothing that needs improvement. But I have. If you allow me, I'd like to go back to that mango grove to meditate.'

Their conversation continued like this for some time, before the Buddha finally relented.

'Meghiya, since you speak so much of meditation, what can I say? Go ahead,' the Buddha said.

As Meghiya settled in for his meditation near the mango grove, he was beset with thousands of thoughts. Most of his thoughts had three particular themes: they were malicious, cruel and lustful. Disappointed by the fact that he had left normal life to become a monk and yet was still experiencing these thoughts, he returned to the Buddha with a heavy heart. Unsurprised by the young monk's experience (I imagine the Buddha rolling his eyes at this point), the Buddha shared with Meghiya five ways to cultivate the freedom of one's heart.

First, you need genuine friendship. Friendship that is built on honesty. Second, live in a way that is ethically responsible. Third, talk about things that inspire your practice. Fourth, have an energy for cultivating goodness in the world. And finally, reflect often on how fleeting life is.

The Buddha continued, 'When there is genuine friendship, there is room for ethical conduct. When there is genuine friendship, you are inspired to practice. When there is genuine friendship, you have the energy to cultivate goodness, and when there is genuine friendship, we can reflect on impermanence more wholly.'

To me, this story describes a special kind of friendship, a spiritual friendship. It's known in Pali, the language of the Buddha, as Kalyāṇa-mitta.

Often we may find we're friends with people because of the school we went to or the college or workplace we were at. Perhaps we met through social events or parties. We tend to have something in common with these friends – we like the same music, dress the same or perhaps follow the same football team. They support us, humour us, listen to us and probably challenge us. Spiritual friendships are no different, but they also bring unexpected people into your life in beautiful ways.

My first teacher, Guruji, had a gorgeous, quaint little studio built from a converted milk bar at the front of his residence. Being drawn to his studio with little to no meditation experience, I vividly remember all the other students in that class. If I had to take a guess, I'd say everyone there was over sixty. There were no fancy yoga leggings or designer meditation gear, just pleasant faces and humble mannerisms. My narcissistic mind was immediately judgemental.

'I would probably never hang out with these people in real life,' I thought.

How wrong I was. I studied with my teacher at that studio for close to a decade, and some of those students became my teachers, friends and even students. I saw people come to this studio as strangers, wrapped up in their own stress and woe, and leave as more wholesome and accepting versions of themselves. Some would arrive on the brink of suicide, spend a few years with my teacher and the community, and leave us as totally different people. I saw strangers become couples, couples become singles and people raise their children around the studio. I made friends who would pass away from cancer. I met people who were millionaires and people who cleaned the studio for free in order to take a class.

This experience taught me that although we often come with our particular set of problems and challenges, what ultimately unites us is the desire to be free from them and to be happy.

Within a community, spiritual friendship isn't always easy. It can be tough, and yet, just as with some of our most genuine friendships, it can be unwavering. Genuine friendship asks us to be accountable. To show up for our friends. And, more importantly, for ourselves. It asks us to be less self-absorbed and more interested in others, which is why we experience so much growth within these friendships.

My eyes were opened when I sat for long hours in meditation classes with some of these people, and when we went on retreat and I heard the stories of those 40 years older than me, who had grown up in different times. Or when I had conversations with teenagers who were brought to the class by their parents. Their stories might have been different, but the essence of what they were saying wasn't. Love, loss, anxiety, confusion and purpose – these were the things we had in common. These are all human qualities that we grapple with over time, and they are all qualities I've grappled with in my life.

The longer we surround ourselves with a community, the more chance there is that we will eventually come up against people

'Who you choose to walk
and grow with is a major part
of life; may they lift you up
in hard times, rejuvenate you
when you are tired and remind
you of how powerful you are.'

– Yung Pueblo

Ultimately, spiritual friendships revolve around honesty, kindness and acceptance, and hopefully alleviate suffering in some small way, shape or form for all involved.

we would normally avoid in our day-to-day life. The kind of people who would get under our skin, who we would simply duck and dodge, or even cancel.

I remember vividly the months of anger I felt towards a particular student who would constantly come to my teacher's class 15–20 minutes late. Every single time. As soon as she took her seat I would look at her and wonder if she felt bad. 'She should,' I often thought to myself.

But these kinds of people often teach us the most valuable lessons. An ability to see ourselves more clearly. To see how worked up and angry we can get over something so inconsequential. Obviously, it wasn't the fact that she was late that bothered me. Most likely it harked back to a time in my childhood when I didn't feel acknowledged or appreciated, and here again, 20-odd years later, someone is again disrespecting 'me'. These moments of insight are the real gifts we receive from our community. The ability to see ourselves a little more clearly.

When you're in a community, you have to work on your responses to these kinds of people and situations. You can't always avoid them in the studio or in your daily life. Over time, you realise that these experiences are really teaching you about how fixed your views on life are, and, more precisely, about how you inadvertently separate yourself from others, or 'other' another person.

Meditation practice has a way of creating space for us to see things clearly, even if we don't like what we see at first. Yes, we are whole and complete AND we have room to grow and learn and navigate our own bad habits and tendencies.

So, how can we bring spiritual friendships into our lives?

We don't always have access to meditation and yoga communities. But we do have the ability to cultivate spiritual friendships with the people already in our lives.

STILL TOGETHER

Cultivate spiritual friendships

Open up

Share with your friends what you're navigating in
your own life. This might be what's coming up for you
in your meditation practice, or in other life situations.

Be vulnerable

Be willing to share yourself honestly. We spend so much
of our time wearing masks, even around the people
who are closest to us. What would it be like to speak our
truth with those we love and trust?

Get to know what motivates your friends

You may be surprised that your friends also have similar
questions to you. Perhaps they are exploring a different
path of practice and have found helpful books. Maybe one
friend is motivated by love and compassion, while another
values purpose and meaning. When was the last time you
really got to know what lights up those in your life?

Talk about your fears

Our fears are as strong as, if not stronger than, our
motivations. When we know what we're running away
from, we may start to understand what we are running
towards. When we know a friend is scared of being alone,
we may begin to understand why they continue to choose
partners that aren't wise for them. When we can see
their hopes and fears, we begin to see the human side
of our friends, and realise that we're not too dissimilar.

Talk about your spiritual paths

We all have our own spiritual path, whether it's an
accountant who finds meaning and purpose through
spreadsheets or a yogi who diligently practises each day.
What's spiritual to us may not be spiritual to everyone.
It's easy to assume that if someone is spiritual, then they're
spiritual like you. But that's not always true, and that's
okay. Our task is to find commonality with all beings,
and to try to really understand them. What can you
glean from your closest friends by knowing what matters
most to them?

PARTNER MEDITATION

Try this meditation for you and your
partner or loved one.

∞

1. Sit quietly and spend a few moments becoming
present – you can use your breath, notice the sounds
or simply notice the sensations of your body.

2. Bring your awareness to your heart. Notice the
physicality of your heart, how you notice it beating,
and your blood pumping. Stay here for a few
moments noticing what arises.

3. Bring to your awareness your partner.
Notice them as if they were there with you now.
Perhaps notice how your energy changes,
if there is a tenderness towards them.

4. Visualise your person happy and joyful, reflecting
on what makes them feel that way. Notice how
you feel as you see this in your heart and mind.
Stay with this for a few minutes.

5. Bring to mind something that your partner has had
to overcome in their life. Perhaps it was a challenging
childhood or a lack of real love in their life. Stay here
for a few minutes.

6. Finally, reflect on the person they are today and
how they show up for the world. Even with everything
they have overcome, they continue to be passionate
and caring and not-perfect, just like you. Stay here
as long as you need.

7. Come back to this practice any time you forget
that your partner is a human being, full of infinite
stories and memories, trying the best they can
with what they have.

STILL TOGETHER

MINDFULNESS AT WORK

I often wonder what my life might look like if I had been introduced to meditation and Buddhism many years earlier. Would I be healthier? Probably. Would I be kinder? Maybe.

What I do know for sure is that I would have saved myself a lot of suffering had I known how to look after my mind and body. When our minds aren't calm, we're at the mercy of our feelings. What a gift it is then, to be able to create space between our stimuli and our (often) habitual responses. Meditation and mindfulness have been shown to improve our ability to concentrate for longer hours with less distraction, improve our mood and be more creative.

But is this the only way to integrate these practices into your work life? Have you, like me, often felt that work life and 'non-work life' were two alternate realities? I felt so free when I was around my friends and family on weekends, but as soon as Monday rolled around, I would mask up and prepare to present a different version of myself. I would be motivated by meaningful connection and authentic experiences on one hand, and fall into bitter office politics on the other.

But what would it look and feel like to make work an extension of your spiritual practice? Here are some suggestions.

Be grateful

Being grateful doesn't mean we have to jump up and down about the things we do at work. It simply means we can take a moment to acknowledge how our work supports our life. For many of us, it's a privilege to be able to use our minds, free of persecution. That's something to be grateful for. Maybe our work creates the conditions that allow us to have a family and feed and clothe them. Or maybe it's as simple as getting to hang out with your work bestie and spend a day in each other's company. When we can recreate the feeling of gratitude in our body, we're already starting our days with positivity. When we meditate, we get to see the ways we are caught up in our own minds, grasping, wanting things to be different and clinging to this idea of separateness. This blocks us from experiencing so much wisdom and satisfaction.

Be intentional

Set an intention as to how you will show up each time you enter your place of work. You could do this after your morning meditation as you're making your way into the office. Instead of thinking about how many things could go wrong that day (our negativity bias), think about how you would like to show up. Would you like to be more courteous to your colleagues today? Maybe you would like to ask for help more. You could even set an intention to take a break every two hours, or simply to remind yourself what you're grateful for. We all know that work days can be unpredictable, but being intentional offers us the chance to be accountable to ourselves.

Be self-aware

Self-awareness is the quality of a leader. And we're all leaders, even if we don't recognise this about ourselves. We all have the power to influence. If we're angry and aggressive towards a friend, they'll be influenced by our actions. Similarly, at work, it's important to be aware of ourselves and our environment. How are our words being perceived? Am I speaking from a place of high emotion? Am I causing myself or another person harm? To answer these questions, we practise mindfulness. We observe ourselves and those around us through their body language and tone. And hopefully, we move through our day skilfully. This means we foster thoughts and actions that create happiness and reduce suffering, instead of the other way around.

STILL TOGETHER

Cultivate tenderness

You may think that work is the least compassionate place there is. You might be right, but what if you're not? A boss of mine would take me out to lunch when she could see that I was struggling. Her simple gesture made me feel less alone and more supported. We have the opportunity to be compassionate when someone is being nasty to us, to think about what might be going on in their lives that might make them act in this way. Maybe they're having health issues or experiencing other pressures. Most importantly, though, we have a powerful opportunity to be compassionate towards ourselves.

Often, we attach a painful narrative to our mistakes, to the things we did (or didn't do) that keep us trapped in a cycle of guilt and shame. It's important to acknowledge the impact of our actions towards ourselves and others, but also to be willing to acknowledge our state of awareness at the time. We could have been having an anxious moment or we might have been lacking sleep. Perhaps we were stressed, or just having a moment when we were not self-aware. There's often a multitude of causes and conditions that explain our actions.

We stay trapped in suffering if we take on the belief that our mistakes are linked to who we are at our core, instead of merely representing a moment in time when we lacked clarity or wisdom. Mistakes can form a powerful springboard that launches us in the direction of living a more compassionate and virtuous life–one that begins with a deep acceptance of our own humanity.

Mindful moments

Take a break. Slow down every now and then. We live in a society where being productive and efficient is what we (and others) are judged on. But we can create within ourselves moments of mindfulness. A walk around the block, taking five deep and meaningful breaths, or stopping to smell your morning coffee can all be moments we disrupt the 'productivity at all costs' mentality.

Create meaning

Constantly ask yourself if your life reflects what you value most. You might be in a job that feels meaningless and dead-end, but it could be a pit stop on a bigger journey. How is the work you're doing creating a life of meaning? Research suggests that those who prioritise meaning in their lives over happiness are more productive. This was true for me. During the first three years of A—SPACE, we were constantly struggling to keep the business afloat. When it all became too much and I thought about throwing in the towel, I would receive a positive email from a student who told me how much the community had supported her through her recovery, or a gift from a six-year-old who attended class with her mother and painted a picture with me in it. These moments gave my life so much meaning, and little moments like these can spark momentum. In my experience, the thing that has created the most meaning is reflecting on how the work I do will help others or, more simply, how the work I do won't create harm.

Questioning our meaning can also open up questions about what we do for work. Is it ethical? Am I hurting anyone? How can I do more to help? The spiritual path is full of difficult self-inquiry. There are no 'correct' answers, we must come to find peace and clarity through our own meditation and reflection, and through the lens of wisdom and compassion.

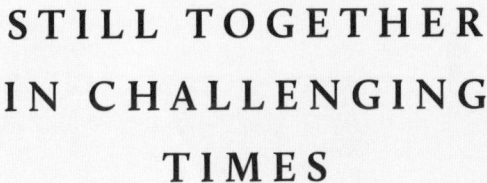

STILL TOGETHER
IN CHALLENGING
TIMES

∞

CHAPTER SIX

∞

New meditators often tell me right in the middle of a crisis that they need to start meditating. This is probably the most challenging time to begin a meditation practice. I would caution against beginning a heavy concentration-based meditation practice if you are experiencing trauma-related anxiety, however, and would not advise anyone to go on a silent meditation retreat right after a significant life event. But meditation can be tremendously beneficial during challenging times if we have the right techniques and the correct approach.

STILL TOGETHER

A WORD ON MEDITATING
DURING CHALLENGES

It's important to remember that there are days when our practice will be tremendously challenging for us. Days where we can't muster the energy to sit, let alone concentrate or focus. It may simply be hard even to function like a normal human being. That's okay. Remember, your meditation practice need not always take place on the cushion. It shows itself in the way you speak to yourself or how you tend to others. If this means you need a day to yourself, so be it. Enjoy yourself fully. While we may prepare ourselves for everything when we meditate, we must also be mindful of being compassionate to our bodies.

TURNING TOWARDS PAIN

A teaching that has supported me immeasurably during the COVID-19 pandemic is the teaching of the Sallatha Sutta, otherwise known as The Arrow.

In one of his many discourses, the Buddha shared that as humans we experience physical, mental or emotional pain as if we were shot by an arrow. Whether that's the ending of a relationship, the loss of a job or simply adjusting to a new way of being, it can be painful and even traumatic. The Buddha said that for us 'uninitiated or run-of-the-mill folks' – i.e. you and me – we know no other response than to resist the pain. We resist it in such a way that we create a story about the arrow in order to make sense of what has happened – but, ultimately, it's simply a way for us to avoid feeling the pain of the arrow.

So we tell ourselves that we deserve to be broken up with, or we get angry at ourselves or the world because we have lost money or we think what has happened is supremely unfair and unjust. All of this resistance adds to our suffering, because in creating a narrative around why we are in pain, we have shot ourselves with a second arrow. This second arrow is what hurts us the most. It is laced with our views about ourselves, our past experiences and conditioning. It leads to catastrophising and worrying, and over time affects our mental health. This is all because we are avoiding the pain of the first arrow.

As humans, we are going to experience the inevitable ups and downs of life. We know we will at some point experience praise and blame, gain and loss, pleasure and sorrow. And yet, we still do everything we can to avoid sorrow. Our stories serve as a way for us to process our suffering, instead of simply being with the hurt and pain. Suffering is suffering – it is inevitable. If we don't allow ourselves to feel the weight of our sadness, it permeates our life in unhelpful ways.

The Buddha says that to navigate challenges, losses and pain, we must begin by not avoiding the pain, sadness, guilt, anger and worry. We must experience the pain of the first arrow, sit with it, tend to it and feel compassion for it, and look at the nature of another impermanent phenomenon – without shooting ourselves with a second arrow. This involves realising that we can accept whatever is arising in our body, like a cloud drifting through the sky. It's okay to experience strong emotions. It's part of being a human.

A MEDITATION FOR DIFFICULT TIMES

Here's a practice you may want to use in challenging times. It is a practice that invites us to sit with and create compassionate space, for whatever arises.

A caveat: if this practice ever gets overwhelming, simply stop, bring awareness to sounds around you or your breath, or simply go for a walk or talk to a friend. The pain is real, but the story doesn't have to be.

This practice will invite us to turn compassionately towards our emotions.

∞

1. Sit in a comfortable position. You can even lie down if you feel comfortable doing so. Just be mindful of not getting too cosy, as you may fall asleep. If you do, don't worry about it – it means you need it.

2. Bring awareness to your body, perhaps starting with the feet, noticing the sensations of your feet as they touch the ground. Notice the legs and anything that they brush up against. Observe your seat and the feeling of it.

3. Gradually move towards your abdomen, stomach and chest. Allow your awareness to simply rest there, becoming aware of what is present, while noticing the physical sensations of what is there.

4. Here you may simply ask yourself a question, 'What is here for me today?'

5. Again, notice what is arising in your body. It may be nothing. It could be your stomach churning. It could even be your heart beating or racing in a certain way.

6. Allow your mind to rest in observing a particular feeling or sensation, perhaps asking again, 'What is here for me today?'

7. Perhaps a strong emotion or feeling arises at this point. Naturally, our mind may want to push this away or, if it's pleasant, to feel more of it. But, here, the invitation is to allow whatever is coming up to come up.

8. Compassionately create space for any feelings to be felt, even if you can't feel anything. You're not pushing away or craving anything, you're being kind to whatever arises. It's here, so it is real.

9. Tend to your feelings like a mother would tend to her crying baby. Be gentle, be warm.

10. End your practice by taking ten deep and slow breaths, breathing down into your stomach and exhaling through the nose into the front or back of your body. Do more if you have the time and space.

STILL TOGETHER

Epilogue

Full disclosure: when I started writing this book I knew that this final chapter would be a call to action for each of us to look at ways we could integrate these teachings into our beautiful, brave and ever-evolving lives in meaningful ways.

Then we experienced the COVID-19 pandemic.

After over a decade of practice, study and teaching, I had a full-blown panic attack. After I had sworn that I would never again put myself in the position of burning out, I burnt out. After teaching so many people to turn towards their anxiety, I did everything I could to avoid my own. And having just written a chapter about the perils of social media, in the midst of lockdown I found that social media was the only thing that gave me comfort.

My world, much like everyone else's, had been turned upside down. My studio ground to a halt, overnight. The gym I went to closed. The highlight of my morning – visiting the local coffee shop around the corner from my house – was no longer available to me. But worse, people were losing their jobs, deaths seemed insurmountable and fighting this invisible enemy seemed futile. And every single one of my conversations was laced with tinges of hopelessness.

As the world became gripped in a state of collective fear, anxiety and trauma, I did what I unconsciously do all the time: I started to over-work. I put together online courses and free classes, checked in on my friends, read more books, listened to more podcasts, began working out at home (twice a day), and, of course, continued to write this book. It was easy for me to rationalise all of this. I had spare time, and this was what my community needed, this offering of mindfulness and meditation, of community and care.

It never occurred to me that I was doubling my usual output in the middle of a global pandemic. Not until one day when I jumped out of the shower, sat down on my bed and broke down crying.

I thought my tears were for others. I thought of my lonely mother, and my black and brown friends in New York who were disproportionately affected by the virus. I missed my girlfriend, whom I had not seen for six months because Australian borders were closed. I wept for my daughter, who was living in a COVID-19 hotspot and was separated from me and her grandmother, my mother. But as I continued to weep, I noticed my body, which was trembling and shaking. I turned towards it with the gentleness of a mother tending to a child that is distressed.

As I did this, what opened up in my body was trauma.

My teacher, Miles, describes trauma as 'a subjective response to an unexpected, unprepared or perceived threat to life or bodily harm to oneself or another'. Up until I started working with Miles, I knew trauma to be 'big T' Trauma – a significant event in a person's life that may have revolved around violence or violation. I knew my immigrant upbringing had been challenging, and I assumed I would have some hang-ups from that. But what was really interesting was reading David Treleaven's excellent book, *Trauma-sensitive Mindfulness*, and learning that trauma can have less to do with the content of an event than with the impact it has on our physiology.

What I was going through was grief and loss. I had lost my way of life. The things that made me feel happy and safe were gone. I was trying to reconcile my own loss and grief while simultaneously navigating hoarding shoppers and feeling an unrelenting need to be productive and to hold space for family and friends.

I was grappling with the feeling that I needed to save my time, my energy, even the space I lived in. The feeling that I was helpless as the world was changing moment to moment. The feeling that I had to be productive in order to feel like I was enough. Maybe, just maybe, the busier I got, the less lonely I would feel.

As I sat on the bed, crying, helpless, confused and cold, it dawned on me that much of what I had practised throughout my life had in fact prepared me to respond to that moment. I knew in my bones that impermanence was a fact of life. I knew how my lower-class upbringing had hardwired me to protect what I had. But I also noticed how society had shaped my conviction that productivity would trump my wellbeing and that if I worked hard enough, I could power through anything. It was complete madness to think that I could produce in the same capacity

I had before COVID-19 hit. But above all, the lesson that moment taught me was to turn towards the pain, allow myself not to be okay and to move towards slowing down.

I remember thinking how revolutionary it was to slow down. To have days where I sat in bed and binge watched *Tiger King*, or just talked on the phone to friends. Inadvertently, in the middle of a pandemic, I relearned what it meant to tend to myself and to recognise I didn't need much to have a good life. I wasn't shopping online, I wasn't eating out every day. My mind, while still anxious, also felt like it was slowing down. And my body started to feel clean again. Importantly, I started to feel like I was in my body.

Sometime after the first wave of the pandemic, I was feeling better than I had in months. The clean eating had paid off, I was fortunate to have space to exercise and my closest friends were within walking distance. Even though my partner was in New York and I missed her terribly, I had somewhat adjusted to a new way of being in the world.

Then Ahmaud Arbery and George Floyd were murdered.

The weeks and months that followed were some of the most challenging in my life. What arose in me was not only the anger at seeing people who looked like me being treated like disposable items, it was also the sudden realisation that racism, something that had been my lived experience, was all of a sudden trending. The dichotomy was that I was happy that racism had finally entered the public lexicon, while simultaneously reckoning with something I had endured silently for decades.

Having had incredibly challenging conversations with those both close to me and far away and seeing the pain of my black and brown friends, I felt my heart break again. But this time the heartbreak was accompanied by another powerful force: anger.

Immobilised by rage, I sat in bed for days, spoke to people I trusted and simply cried. This time, I struggled to meditate, to teach online classes and even to finish this book.

But what followed in those weeks was a starkly different response to the one I had in the early stages of COVID-19. I felt the anger pushing me towards action. This was the moment we had been waiting for, I realised, and the moment I had been practising meditation for. This was a moment for liberation.

If our mindfulness practice aims to liberate us from suffering, then we have to acknowledge that our suffering, yours and mine, is intertwined. If you suffer, I suffer; if I do, you inadvertently do. This is not simply poetic, it's based on the philosophy of interconnection that COVID-19 demonstrated. If a pathogen can cause suffering in China and we simply think it is a Chinese problem, we suffer. But if we can be moved to treat another person's suffering as if it were our own, the impact we can have is limitless.

Every action begins with a thought; the idea of separateness is a construct of the mind. And our meditation and yoga practice can no longer be separate from the wellness of those around us.

We can't downward dog or meditate this moment away; we never could. Love and light will not dismantle systemic racism. Neither will avoiding the topic because it's 'heavy energy' or 'low vibration' or 'not on brand'. We're at a key juncture in our lives where genuine change can and will take place, if we're prepared to do the work to transform, both individually and collectively.

Transformation is more than a momentary black square on Instagram or a shout-out to favourite black and brown authors. It is long, hard and, mostly, ungratifying work that will continue to break your heart. But that doesn't mean we should stop.

Being a meditator shouldn't discourage us from being active in speaking up about structures that continue to divide us. When we're guided by ending suffering for all beings, we can use the power of our anger and our heartbreak to cut through our own ignorance and that of the world around us. And if our motivations are rooted in understanding, compassion and altruism, then our practice is not only compatible with our activism, it fortifies it.

My anger gave way to compassion. But first it broke me open, and perhaps it did so for the rest of the world, too. The invitation throughout this book has been to cultivate clear seeing and, along the way, to uproot greed, hatred and ignorance so that you may free yourself from suffering. Your awareness will deepen along the way, along with your compassion – but what will you do with it?

The Zen Buddhist master Thich Nhat Hanh coined the phrase Engaged Buddhism, a movement of individuals connecting their practice to global ethics and social action. 'Meditation means to be aware of what is happening in the present moment – to your body, to your feelings, to your environment,' he said in an interview with *Tricycle* magazine. 'But if you see and if you don't do anything, where is your awareness? Then where would your enlightenment be?'

Rather than being overwhelmed by our anger, we can learn to befriend it, harness it and be propelled by it. And our meditation practice then becomes a tool of sustenance and regeneration. One that we use to remind ourselves that our deepest connection to ourselves, each other and our environment has always been there. And just as we have learned to divide ourselves, we can unlearn the very same thing.

Perhaps it's in stillness that we come together. Perhaps it's in togetherness that we become still enough to recognise what really matters, and what we can do to encourage the wellbeing of not just ourselves, but of our friends, family, lovers, friends, neighbours and complete strangers.

'Because you are alive,
everything is possible.'

– Thich Nhat Hanh

Sit in the messiness, the uncertainty, the hopes and fears, cultivate your equanimity. This is what you've been practising for.

The unpredictability of life

Uncertainty is as much a part of our human experience as breathing. We can get lost in the grip of fear and our attachment to certainty, or we can nurture and care for ourselves and each other amid the worry.

During times of upheaval, it can be beneficial to regulate your nervous system, take deep breaths and take refuge in your mindfulness and spiritual practice. Finally, think of all the other people who are feeling what you're feeling right now. If the world at times feels too overwhelming, give yourself some space. These are the moments we practise for.

STILL TOGETHER

Acknowledgements

It turns out that writing a book during a global pandemic and a social revolution is harder than I thought. For this very reason I'd like to thank those who helped me maintain my sanity, and to those who guided me along the ride to bring this work to light.

First, I'd like to thank my teachers. Guruji, Channa, none of this could have been possible without you and I am profoundly grateful, as you embraced and forever changed my life. Your teachings on compassion and generosity transformed my direction and for those whom I have had the privilege to teach. To Dr. Miles Neale and Scott Tusa, thank you both for your fervent and authentic teachings in Tibetan Buddhism – you arrived serendipitously into my life and both taught me about the intersections of our spiritual practice with modern life, I thank you for this. Anu Gupta, my friend and my brother, I am grateful for our karmic bond. To the Theravada monks and nuns in Sri Lanka, you have my heart – whenever I hear your chants I am transported home. To my exceptional family, Amma, Thatha and Gayan, you are also my home and I love you.

Sophie-Alexia, my love, my unofficial editor and best friend, thank you for putting up with me.

Annabel Ross and Caroline Clements, thanks for making sure this book made sense! And to the wonderful team at Hardie Grant, especially you, Alice – thank you for believing in me and this project. My wonderful friend and agent Cecile Barendsma, thank you for your confidence and support in designing and seeing through a true and honest piece that would honour our practice.

Thank you to those who have been here in the big and the small ways, every show of support has made this possible. To my future readers, let's ride this journey together.

About the author

Since first being introduced to the magic of meditation decades ago and embarking on his own journey to become a teacher, Manoj has helped thousands of people to embrace stillness of mind and body, enabling them to live fearlessly on the path to a happier and more meaningful life.

His teaching and practice is informed by Buddhist philosophy, psychology and social justice principles, with an emphasis on promoting diversity and inclusion in the wellness space.

After training under renowned teachers Dr Miles Neale, Channa Dassanayaka and Joe Loizzo, Manoj has based himself between the US and Australia for the past five years, teaching meditation and mindfulness across both continents.

In 2015 he founded A-SPACE, Australia's first drop-in meditation studio, in Melbourne, and in 2020 he became the co-founder of Open, a California-based wellness platform incorporating meditation, movement, music, sound healing and breathwork. He is also the co-founder of the Australian/New Zealand arm of EVRYMAN, a men's emotional intelligence movement; Australia's first global ambassador for international wellness apparel company Lululemon; and is among the most sought-after teachers and public speakers in the world.

Manoj's proudest achievement of all is his daughter, Taylah.

Published in 2021 by Hardie Grant Books,
an imprint of Hardie Grant Publishing

Hardie Grant Books (Melbourne)
Building 1, 658 Church Street
Richmond, Victoria 3121

Hardie Grant Books (London)
5th & 6th Floors
52–54 Southwark Street
London SE1 1UN

hardiegrantbooks.com

 A catalogue record for this
book is available from the
National Library of Australia

Still Together
ISBN 9781743796719

10 9 8 7 6 5 4 3 2 1

Commissioning Editor: Alice Hardie-Grant
Editor: Vanessa Lanaway
Design Manager: Mietta Yans
Designer: Studio Terra | Vanessa Masci
Illustrators: Sacrée Frangine | Célia Amroune and Aline Kpade
Production Manager: Todd Rechner

Colour reproduction by Splitting Image Colour Studio
Printed in China by Leo Paper Products LTD.

Hardie Grant acknowledges the Traditional Owners of the country on which we work,
the Wurundjeri people of the Kulin nation and the Gadigal people of the Eora nation,
and recognises their continuing connection to the land, waters and culture. We pay our
respects to their Elders past, present and emerging.

 The paper this book is printed on is certified against the
Forest Stewardship Council® Standards and other sources.
FSC® promotes environmentally responsible, socially beneficial
and economically viable management of the world's forests.

'Manoj Dias is a leader amongst the new generation of serious meditators that will carry the torch of the Buddha's teachings into the future. What's special about Manoj is the depth of his practice. It is clearly reflected in the way he lives his life and the way he effectively teaches people how to reclaim their power by walking the path of liberation. *Still Together* is the exact medicine that we need in these times of great change. Whoever takes this book to heart will experience a profound transformation.'

—Yung Pueblo, author of *Inward*

'One of the clearest books on meditation, and our growing need for connection, that I have ever come into contact with. Manoj Dias provides us with a way in that we can all understand, amidst the ever-changing and unpredictable landscape of this planet. *Still Together* is like freshwater, a joy, a needed breath.'

—Yrsa Daley-Ward, author of *Bone*

'One of the kindest and most accessible meditation teachers out there, Manoj Dias has written the book for the world we live in. Full of Buddhist wisdom, hope, and humour, this book will cheer you up and open your heart.'

—Lodro Rinzler, author of *The Buddha Walks Into a Bar*